SECRET TEWKESBURY

David Elder

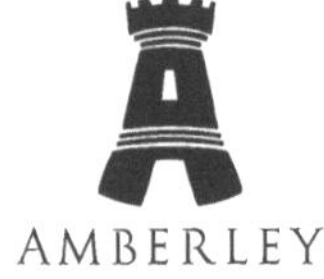

AMBERLEY

About the Author

David Elder read Modern Languages at Bristol University and then, after training as an Information Specialist, enjoyed a career in central government. Now retired, he is the author of several books on Cheltenham, Gloucester, Tewkesbury, Gloucestershire and the Cotswolds, as well as some biographies and plays. As an award-winning photographer he often illustrates his books. You can find out more about David's writing and photography from his website – www.davidelder.net.

For Steph, Kev and Chloe

First published 2023

Amberley Publishing
The Hill, Stroud
Gloucestershire, GL5 4EP

www.amberley-books.com

ISBN 978 1 3981 1186 8 (print)
ISBN 978 1 3981 1187 5 (ebook)

British Library Cataloguing in Publication Data.
A catalogue record for this book is available from the
British Library.

Origination by Amberley Publishing.
Printed in Great Britain.

Appointed GPSR EU Representative: Easy Access
System Europe Oü, 16879218
Address: Mustamäe tee 50, 10621, Tallinn, Estonia
Contact Details: gpsr.requests@easproject.com, +358
40 500 3575

Contents

Introduction

One of the challenges when conducting research into Tewkesbury relates to the variations in the town's spelling. The antiquarian John Leland, for example, used as many as twelve variants within a few pages of his *Itinerary* (1535–43). In doing so, he cast doubt over whether its place name derived from Theoc, a Northumbrian hermit who founded organised religion here in the seventh century, or from the confluence between the rivers Severn and Avon, an area which was once known as Tweoneaum, which means 'between the rivers'. Whichever is correct, a survey of the literature needs to review in particular the occurrences of its Saxon and medieval name of Theocsbury, as well as the use of Tewxbury, later Tewkesbury, which dates from the beginnings of the modern age. Secondly, one feels cautioned to adhere to the correct pronunciation of the modern place name, 'Tooksbury' being considered a 'vulgar sound' according to one authoritative source appearing in the 1820s (see p. 80).

From the historian's point of view it is fortunate that so much of Tewkesbury's unique past, particularly its medieval heritage, has been preserved. Although some urban redevelopment has taken place, it has mostly been small scale and necessarily constrained by the town's rivers and the regular floods that they bring. While much of the town's fascinating history has been documented, there is still much – as Donald Rumsfeld might say – that fits into a category of 'unknown knowns', i.e. facts and truths we already understand and have probably documented somewhere but that we fail to fully appreciate because they lie hidden, neglected, or fragmented across disparate sources. The purpose of this book is to unearth these lost, forgotten, or neglected facts and true stories and unveil interesting new dimensions about the history of this remarkable town.

After providing an overview of Tewkesbury's history, from Neolithic times to the present day, I focus attention on some of the characters who have made an unusual impact in the town – from the thirteenth-century abbot, Alan of Tewkesbury, to the first (former) woman candidate to attempt to run for US President. This is followed by themed chapters covering lesser-known aspects of the town's history focused on crime and punishment, trade and industry, transport, leisure and entertainment, and Tewkesbury's literary connections. The fact that the town has two crossroads with burials, or that Tewkesbury once took part in the clandestine tobacco industry might surprise some, while the fact that mid-nineteenth-century stagecoaches completed the journey to Cheltenham in just thirty minutes, or that the first time Lancashire and Yorkshire played cricket outside their counties was at the Swilgate may impress others. Moreover, a place which contains such a concentrated assortment of interesting and unique heritage also reveals a wealth of fascinating curiosities, some examples of which are included in the final chapter. Whether it is the story of Tewkesbury's concealed shoe or the tale of its 'heroic' Antarctic dog, I hope I have succeeded in creating more 'known knowns' about this unique town.

1. From Theocsbury to Tewkesbury

Although Tewkesbury dates from at least Saxon times when the town was known as Theocsbury, evidence of even earlier occupation exists. A Neolithic settlement in the present-day Oldbury area was probably first established around 2500 BC when local gravel deposits made it an attractive site. Subsequently occupied by the Bronze Age Beaker people, as evidenced by a burial dating from *c.* 1800 BC, it is thought Oldbury subsequently became the centre of a small Roman settlement that thrived because of the well-drained, fertile soil above its gravel beds. Another Roman settlement existed at the Mythe. Either the Romans or the Saxons probably built the Mythe Tute, the man-made mound constructed of red marl, around half of which has now been eroded by the Severn. It was possibly used as a lookout point to warn against the approach of Danish raiders travelling up from the Bristol Channel. Indeed, it is thought the Mythe witnessed skirmishes during the ninth century between King Alfred the Great and the Danes.

The Mythe is also believed to be the site of an early monastery, founded *c.* AD 715, which, around 1102, was then replaced by the present-day abbey in its current location. While Saxon estates and defences existed in or around the Oldbury area of Tewkesbury, it was not until the twelfth century, with the founding of the abbey by Robert Fitzhamon, that Tewkesbury's centre became re-established, gravitating away from Oldbury towards the abbey's precincts. Given the confines imposed by the rivers and their floodplain, significant expansion after the medieval period proved impossible. Within two centuries the town's layout was established: with three principal thoroughfares connecting through narrow alleyways to buildings behind the street façades and this remained largely unchanged until the nineteenth century, as shown in an 1835 map.

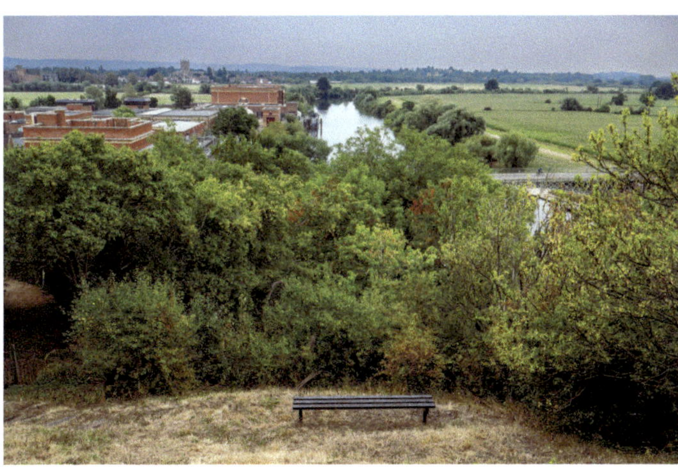

View from the Mythe Tute
looking south.

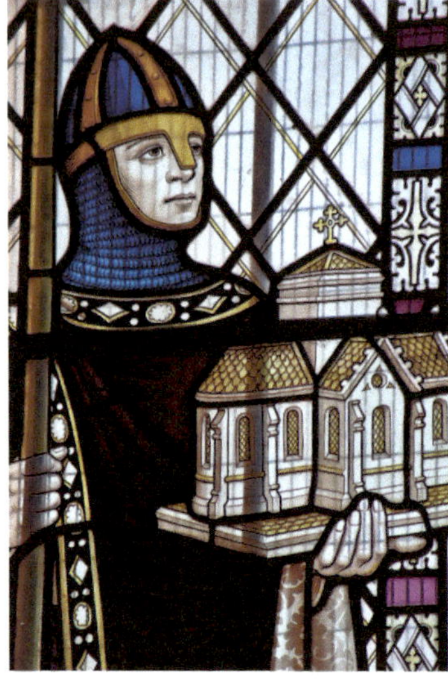

Detail from the abbey's Lady Chapel showing Robert Fitzhamon, the abbey's founder.

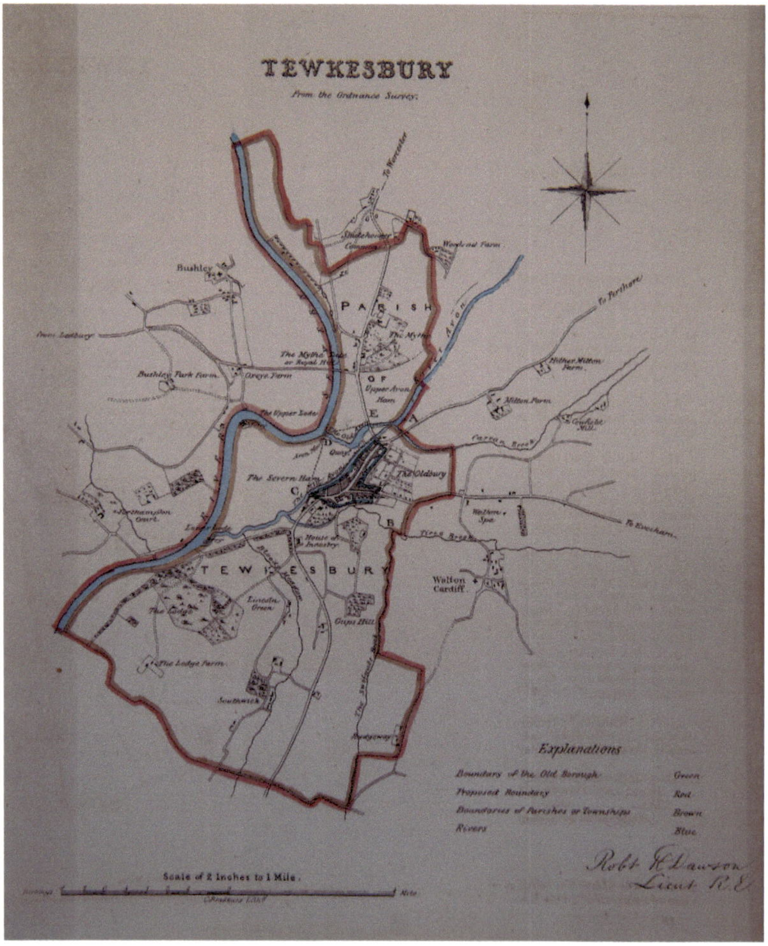

1835 map of Tewkesbury.

From at least the eleventh century, agriculture had become established as the town's main industry. In 1066, for example, it was recorded that Tewkesbury manor 'comprised a large demesne farm supporting 12 ploughs and worked by 50 male and female serfs'. Fishing also formed an important part of the local economy, the Domesday Book listing a fishery at Tewkesbury, and records dating from 1205 indicating the provision of salmon and lampreys for the Crown. A market, originally focused at the High Cross, between High Street and Church Street, was established by William the Conqueror's queen Matilda (1031–83), which brought in annual revenues of 11s 8d from rents and tolls. In 1199 Tewkesbury held its first recorded fair, granted by King John and, as indicated by a plaque, probably held near the corner of Church Street and Gander Lane. By 1790 the town was entitled to hold seven fairs, including its Mop Fair, which continues to the present day – originally a hiring fair for labourers granted by James I in 1609.

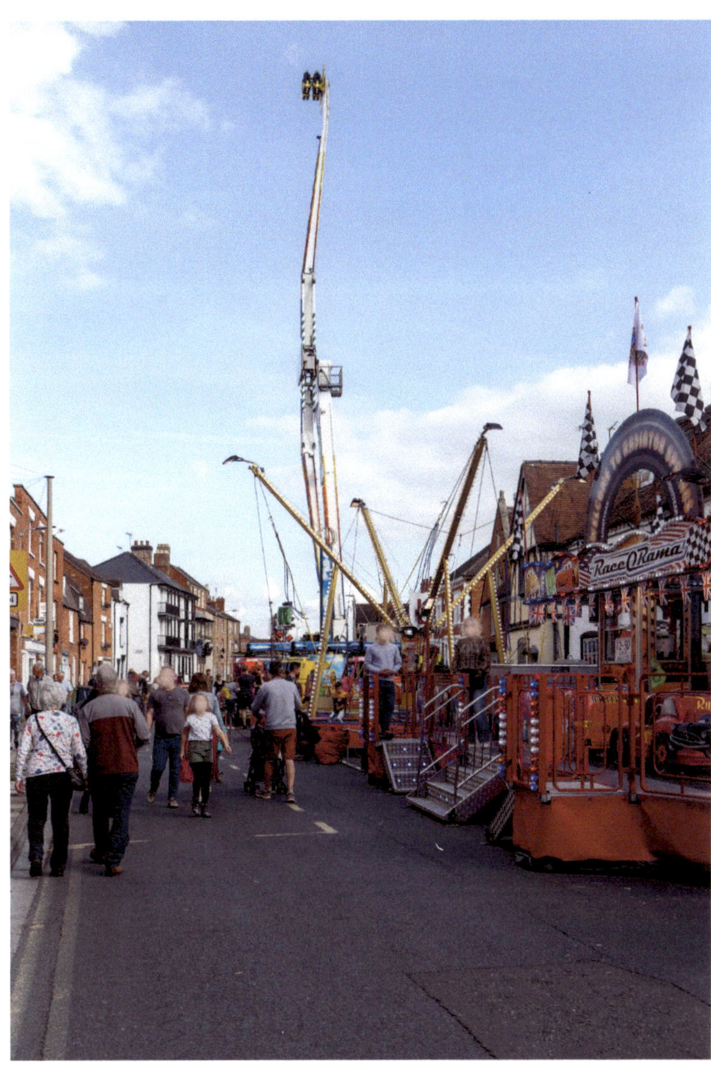

The Mop Fair today.

Apart from its market, from 1102, Tewkesbury became dominated by the abbey until its dissolution in 1540. The abbey's influence is perhaps still visible through the cutting of the Mill Avon, a leat which joins the Avon with the Severn (unless, as some suggest, this was constructed earlier by the Saxons, or even the Romans). Certainly, by the twelfth century the abbey's Benedictine monks had used the Mill Avon to introduce flour milling as one of Tewkesbury's earliest industries, later celebrated through the pages of Mrs Craik's famous novel *John Halifax, Gentleman* (1856). The abbey also became intertwined with the town's most significant historical event: the Battle of Tewkesbury.

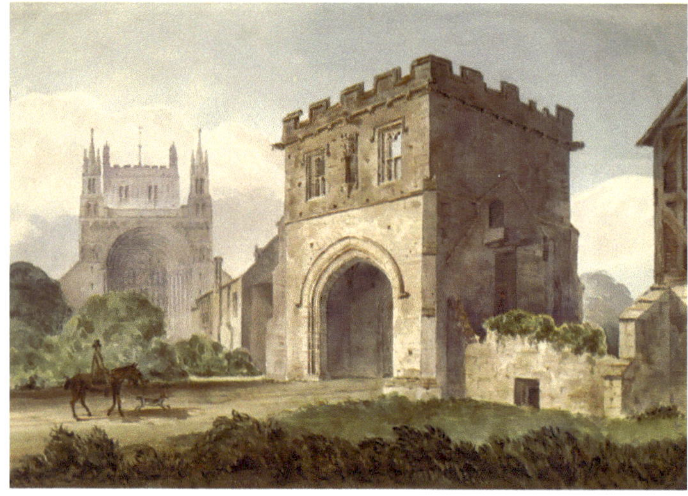

Left: Tewkesbury Abbey by Charles Alban Buckler.

Below: The abbey mill.

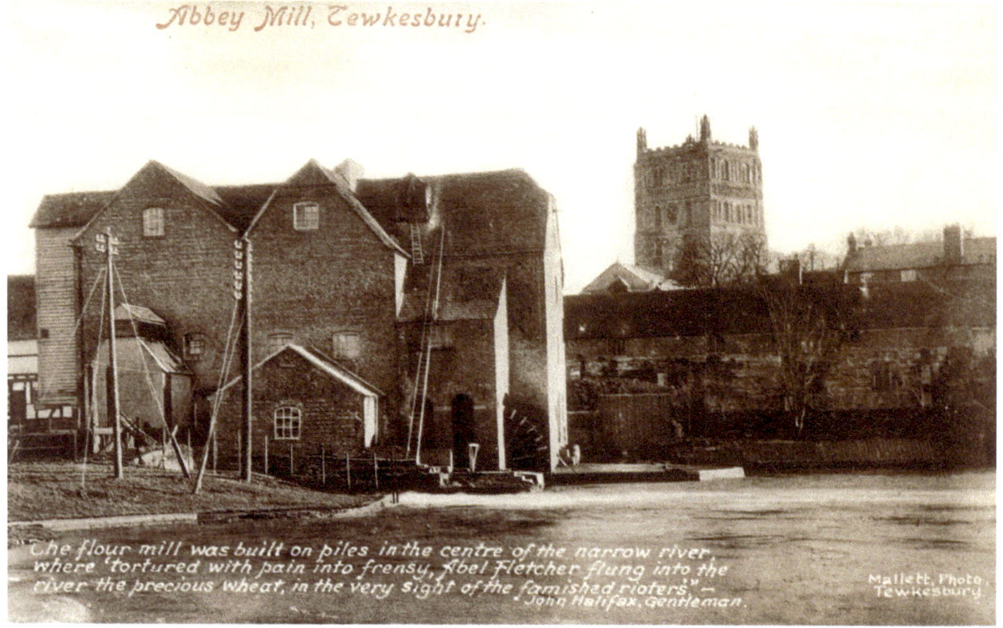

Although Tewkesbury was the scene of minor skirmishes during the Civil War, it was the battle fought on 4 May 1471 that became one of the most significant events in England's history. It resulted in a crushing defeat for the Lancastrian cause, espoused by Margaret of Anjou and her son Edward, Prince of Wales, and a decisive victory for the Yorkist forces, led by King Edward IV, Richard, Duke of Gloucester, and Lord Hastings. The battle was significant not only for its political outcomes, paving the way indirectly for the start of the Tudor dynasty, but also for the savagery of the conflict. It resulted in a significant number of Lancastrian deaths on three sites, one of which later became known as 'Bloody Meadow', and the public execution in the town of several leading Lancastrian noblemen. Over 550 years later, Tewkesbury still recalls the battle, either through the Arrivall sculptures, which provide a striking point of entry for visitors travelling to the town from the south, its annual re-enactment as part of Tewkesbury's medieval festival – the largest of its kind in Europe – or through information boards and a well-signed battle trail that records the terrible events. During the battle the abbey played a significant role, not only providing (temporary) sanctuary for the fleeing Lancastrian noblemen but also their final resting place after their bodies were transferred either from the battlefield or from their place of execution.

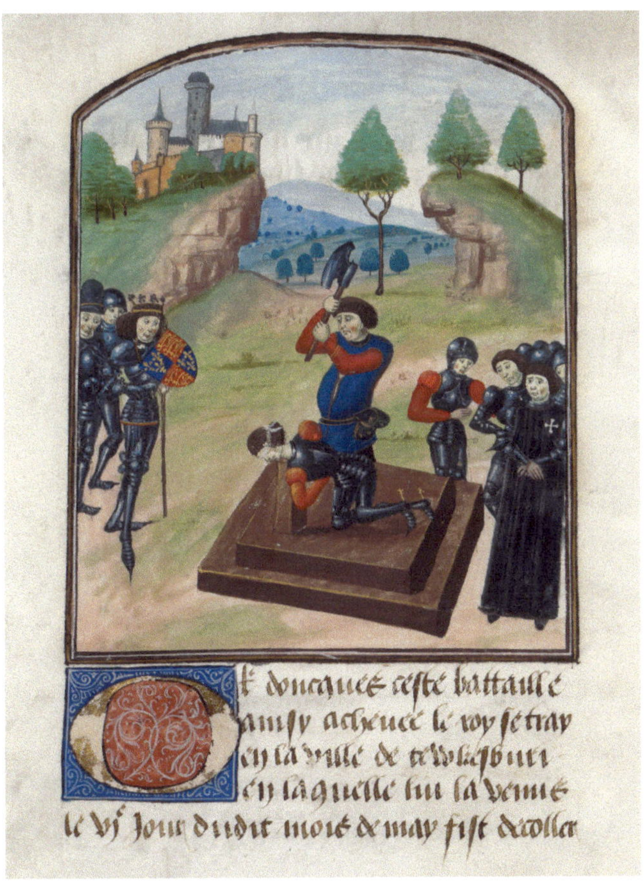

Execution of the Lancastrian Sir Edmund Beaufort after the battle.

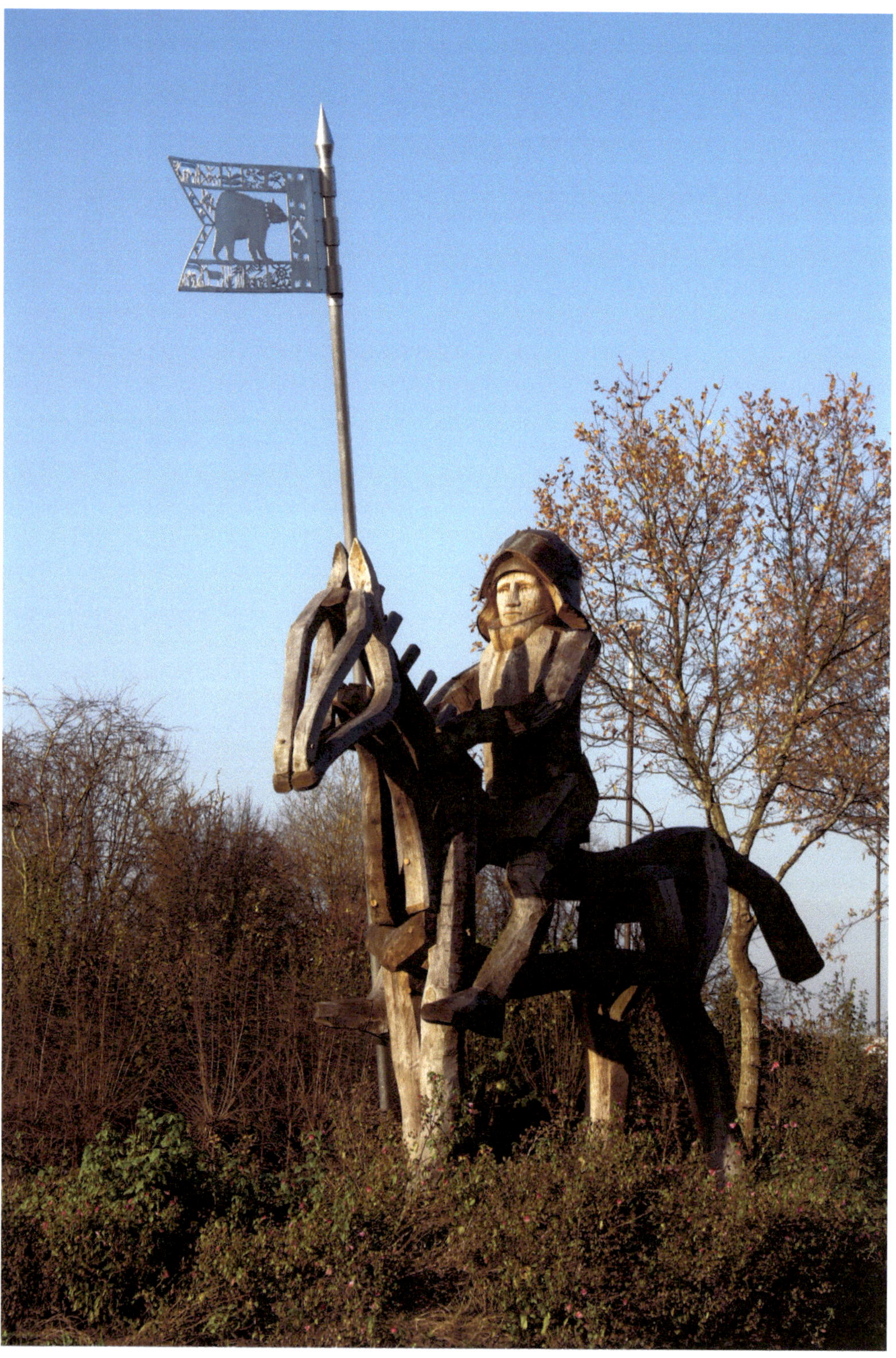

The Arrivall sculpture depicting 'Victory' on the A38 approach towards Tewkesbury.

In the mid-sixteenth century, Tewkesbury's population numbered approximately 1,600. By then, following the dissolution, the abbey had narrowly avoided destruction following a plan by its worthy citizens to rescue it through petitioning the king for permission to purchase it for £453 – this being the value of the bell metal and roof lead. In this way it was able to continue as a parish church, although, on Easter Day 1559, its spire, which once surmounted its tower, caused dismay when it was blown down during divine service.

DID YOU KNOW?
The Oldbury, whose name derives from 'bury' or old fortified place, originally referred to a 70-acre field east of High Street, and north of Barton Street, once occupied by the Romans. Its importance is reflected in the fact that the present High Street was previously called Oldbury Street. There is even speculation that Oldbury formed part of Argistillum, as yet an unidentified Roman settlement that existed between Gloucester and Droitwich. It is thought that the name Argistillum may mean 'white and gleaming', which possibly refers to the town's shiny appearance during times of flood.

In 1575 Tewkesbury was formally incorporated as a borough, giving the council the power to govern the town through a charter granted by Elizabeth I. Challenging times soon descended on Tewkesbury though when it suffered significant outbreaks of the plague. Although this had been an ever-present danger since the first outbreaks of the Black Death in the fourteenth century when a third of the country's population probably perished, in 1578, as many as thirty Tewkesburians died within just six weeks. At first the policy of isolating households seemed to work as only ten plague-related deaths were recorded the following year. Nevertheless, the plague returned in November 1592, initially affecting one or two houses in Barton Street. However, over the following eighteen months it went on to infect 150 houses and caused 560 deaths, around one third of the town's population. During this time the town was barred from attending markets and fairs and had to rely on donated money and produce to avoid further deaths. A further outbreak in 1598 claimed forty lives, while the last incidence probably occurred in 1624 when only twenty people died.

Among the town's most notable events during the seventeenth century was a visit made by George Fox (1624–91), the founder of the Religious Society of Friends, better known as the Quakers. In 1655, his journal recorded that he held a 'great meeting' in Tewkesbury. After being challenged by one of the local parish ministers to see which of them could turn 'a great rabble of rude people' towards 'the divine Light' it was Fox who claimed eventual victory. He made two further visits, in 1660 and 1678. By 1670 the Quakers had converted three houses in St. Mary's Lane, two of which (Nos 16 and 18) still exist, into a Friends' meeting house. Additionally, they created a burial ground on the site of a former barn, directly behind the houses, which, following restoration work by the

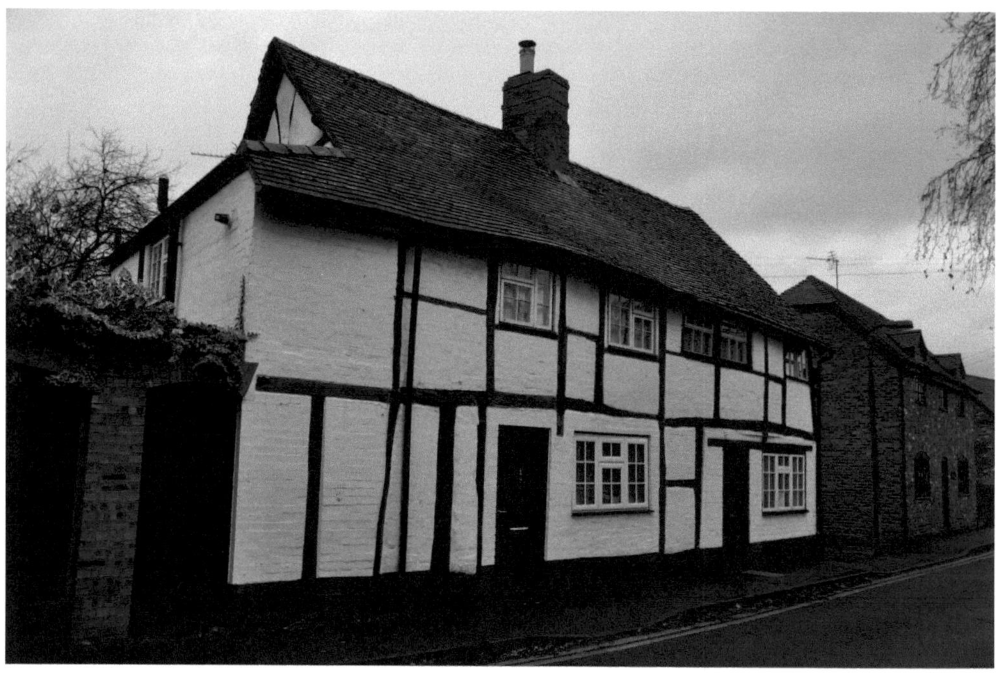

The two houses that once served as the Friends' meeting house.

local Girl Guides for Elizabeth II's visit in 1971, can still be enjoyed by visitors. By 1750 the number of Quakers in the town was estimated at fifty. Although Quaker numbers steadily increased until the beginning of the nineteenth century when a new meeting house in Barton Street was built – now converted into the George Watson Memorial Hall, where part of the original gallery survives – thereafter the Quaker population began to decline.

During the eighteenth century, the town was also influenced by the Methodist movement following the visit by its co-founder, John Wesley, who made several visits to the town from the 1760s to 1780s. On one occasion he even waded through floodwaters to reach his congregation, and in 1775 he considered Tewkesbury to be 'the liveliest place in the circuit'. Another important visitor was King George III, who toured the town on two occasions in July 1788 during his stay in Cheltenham where he drank the waters for a possible cure of his illness. After visiting the Mythe Tute (sometimes called Royal Hill following the visit), where the king and queen fell on their hands after the steep climb, they toured the abbey. Later, when entertained by the High Steward of Tewkesbury, the king passed beneath a triumphal arch of flowers that was temporarily constructed near the Swan (now occupied by Peacocks, No. 10 High Street). Impressed by his affability, the townsfolk were also interested to learn about the king's interest in farming. However, despite showing interest in buying one of the town's local horses and some Tewkesbury sheep, the latter proved too large for George's purpose and the former too dear.

Seven years later, on 24 June 1795, Tewkesbury witnessed one of its most significant riots when around 200 people protested against the high prices of wheat flour. They were also objecting to the profiteering practices of producers and therefore decided to steal the

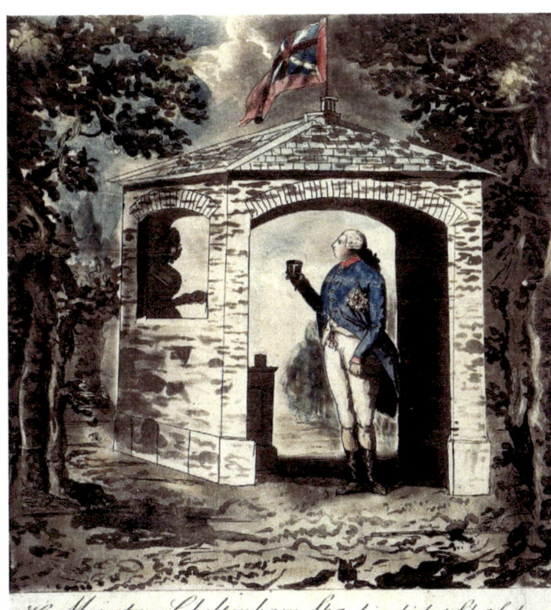

King George III taking the waters at Cheltenham.

flour, which was being loaded into barges at the quay for transportation to Birmingham to secure premium prices. These disturbances, sometimes described as 'the revolt of the housewives', were typically led by women. In Tewkesbury's case it was five women, who were brought to trial as the ringleaders: Hester Macmaster, Mary Aldridge, Sarah Kinson, Ann Mayall, and Happy Fielder. They were found guilty and each served six months' sentences in Gloucester Gaol.

DID YOU KNOW?
The well-known story of the Tewkesbury Jew who died after falling into a privy may simply have arisen as an urban myth, which was commonplace during the Middle Ages. The man supposedly lived in Elmbury in 1259, and died after refusing to be rescued on Saturday, the day of his Sabbath. It was also said that Richard de Clare, Earl of Gloucester, likewise forbade him to be rescued on Sunday, the Christian Sabbath, thus how he came to be found dead by Monday morning.

The ability to control the spread of infectious diseases in Tewkesbury was not helped by the crowded housing development in the town's alleyways. These began to be constructed from medieval times, partly in response to the shortage of building land and partly as a means for the property owner to generate income. Over the years the alleys have assumed different names, reflecting their different ownership or trading focus. Hughes' Alley, for example, which leads from Barton Street to Swilgate Road, is named after a dairyman, Joe Hughes, who kept cows in his meadow on Perry Hill. It has been appropriately commemorated through decorative artwork by Lezli Lawrence at the entrance to the alley. This includes an elm tree, which once existed in Hughes' meadow, and is thought to be the place where George Whitefield – probably in 1739 (see p. 32) – and, later, John Wesley preached. Yarnell's Alley, on the other hand, was named after a chair maker of that name, remembered for being a strong supporter of the French Revolution.

In 1832, the town was visited by a severe cholera epidemic. Despite the affected households being issued with chloride of lime by the Board of Health to fumigate the germs seventy-six lives were lost, a quarter of whom were under ten years of age. Another epidemic followed in 1849, leading to a further fifty-four deaths. These events are commemorated by a monument in the town's cemetery which overlooks a burial pit, where 108 of the 130 victims were laid to rest. Such was the poor state of the town around this time that Tewkesbury was reputedly declared 'the dirtiest town in the kingdom'. In 1850 one of the town's surgeons William Key Tunnicliffe summarised some the town's most significant public health concerns:

> I attribute the spread of fever in these alleys to their confined situation, causing want of ventilation, and their crowded state. Of course the filthy condition of these alleys would tend to increase the disease. No doubt the health of the town would be improved by the introduction of proper privy accommodation, combined with a good system of drainage and water-supply. I attribute the high mortality of Tewkesbury, in part, to the low situation of the town, and the floods to which the country surrounding it is exposed.

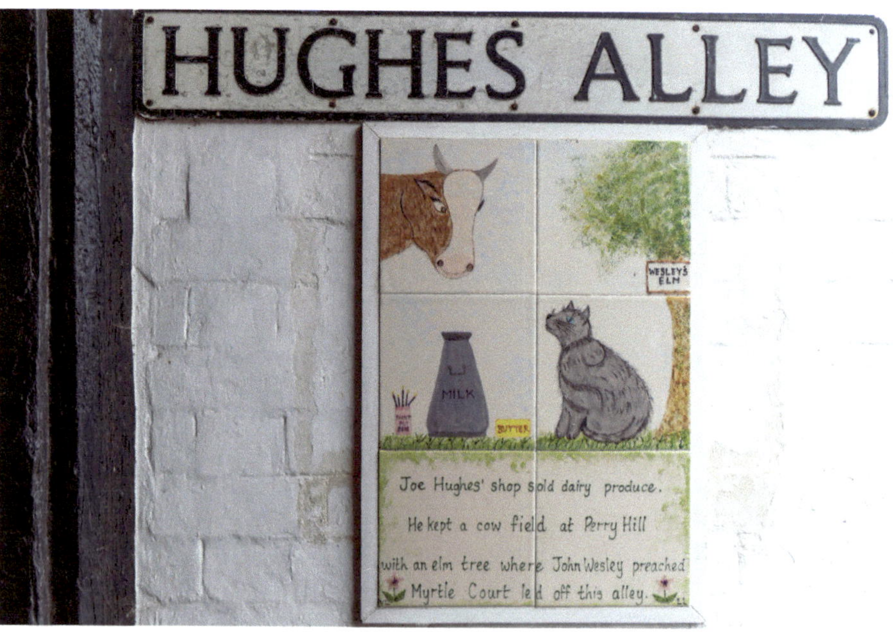

Artwork commissioned by Project Alleycat in Hughes' Alley.

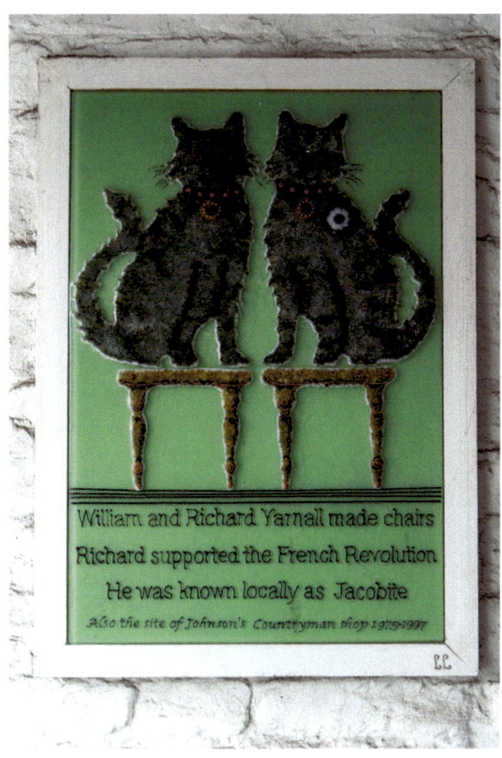

Artwork commissioned by Project Alleycat in Yarnell's Alley.

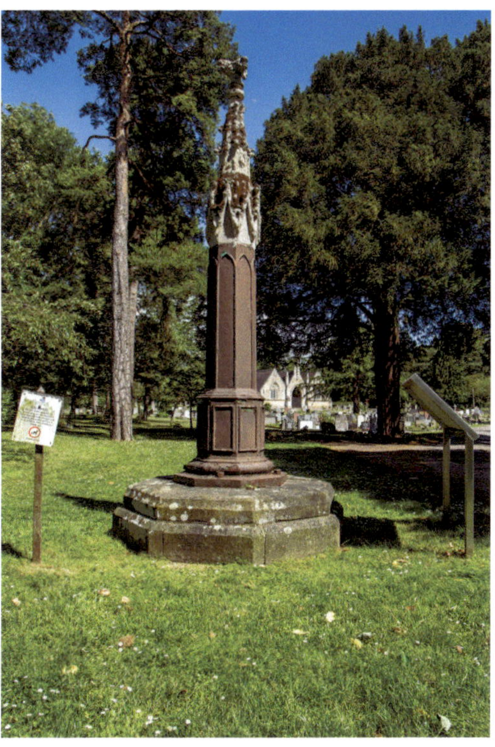

Monument to the cholera epidemic.

While slum clearance and redevelopment in the town's alleyways followed, reducing the alleys that once numbered ninety to just thirty today, their unique heritage is being kept alive through community groups, such as Project Alleycat, also known as Tewkesbury Alley Revival (TAR), which promotes interest in and revival of these intriguing passageways. Throughout its entire development Tewkesbury has been significantly constrained through its physical geography, perhaps most markedly illustrated by the contrast in fortunes during the nineteenth century when the town's one-time smaller neighbour Cheltenham became nine times larger than Tewkesbury within 100 years. Although many changes have occurred, particularly regarding new trades and industries practised in the town, much has stayed the same. On 27 January 1970, for example, the town showed the continuing importance of the agricultural trade to its prosperity when around 175 farm tractors, cattle trucks, trailers, private cars and vans gridlocked the town's streets. Arriving at The Cross from three directions, a similar scene might have taken place a thousand years ago.

Another part of the continuum has been the cycle of disease, suffering and death, which revisited the town from 2020 following the outbreak of the Coronavirus pandemic. The data collected on 28 October 2021 recorded Tewkesbury as having the UK's highest infection rate of 831.1 per 100,000. While the total number of deaths recorded so far – defined as the number of people whose death certificate mentioned COVID-19 as one of the causes – is comparatively much lower than the 33 per cent rate experienced during the plague of 1592–94, the 235 deaths registered so far up to 17 June 2022 suggest a similar 2 per cent death rate to the cholera epidemics that devastated the town during the early nineteenth century.

DID YOU KNOW?
A needle maker called Mr Lewis, who lived in Wilkes' Alley, was crowned Louis, the eighteenth king of France, in June 1814, following Napoleon's abdication and exile to Elba. The ceremony formed part of the town's celebrations of peace and included hanging an effigy of the defeated emperor from gallows erected opposite the Black Bear. John Rogers, author of a book about the town's alleys, knew 'King Lewis (Louis)' – originally written by Rogers as 'Lemes' – and recalled the speech he made from the Town Hall balcony, 'thanking them for restoring him to the throne of his forefathers and promising to reign righteously in the future'.

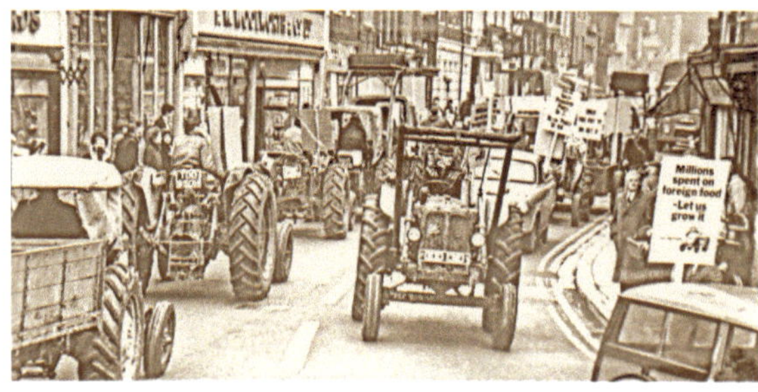

The farmers' protest of 1970.

2. Local Characters

Over the years many local characters have entered the town's folklore. Ellen ('Nellie') Jones, for example, a shopkeeper at the upper end of the High Street, proudly recalled kicking the soapbox from under the feet of Sir Oswald Mosley, leader of the British Union of Fascists. Mosley was giving a speech at an open-air rally in Quay Street during the 1930s, trying to drum up support for his 'Blackshirts', but, after that, he never returned to Tewkesbury. Through the ages other characters have made their mark too – from wise abbots to town criers, distinguished ordinary seamen to miserly tanners and reputedly the first (former) woman candidate to attempt to run for US President.

Alan of Tewkesbury (d. 1202)
Among the ancient tombs in the abbey is a coffin lid of black Purbeck marble inscribed with the words 'DOMINUS ALANUS ABBAS', commemorating the twelfth-century abbot, Alan. The tomb was opened in 1795, initially revealing an apparently well-preserved body, almost 600 years old, but which, after being exposed to the air, soon crumbled away. While his physical remains disintegrated his remarkable story is well preserved through contemporary accounts. Believed to have been born in England, it is known that Alan had been a canon at Benavento in southern Italy before becoming a Benedictine monk at Canterbury and then, in 1179, its prior. Significantly, following the murder of the archbishop Thomas Becket by King Henry II's supporters in 1170, an event probably witnessed by Alan according to the local historian James Bennett, he was entrusted with arranging the letters associated with the controversy surrounding Becket and the king.

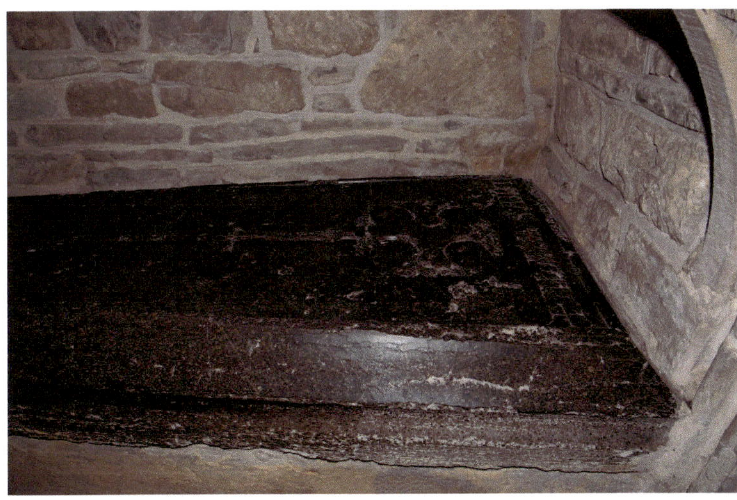

The tomb of Alan of Tewkesbury.

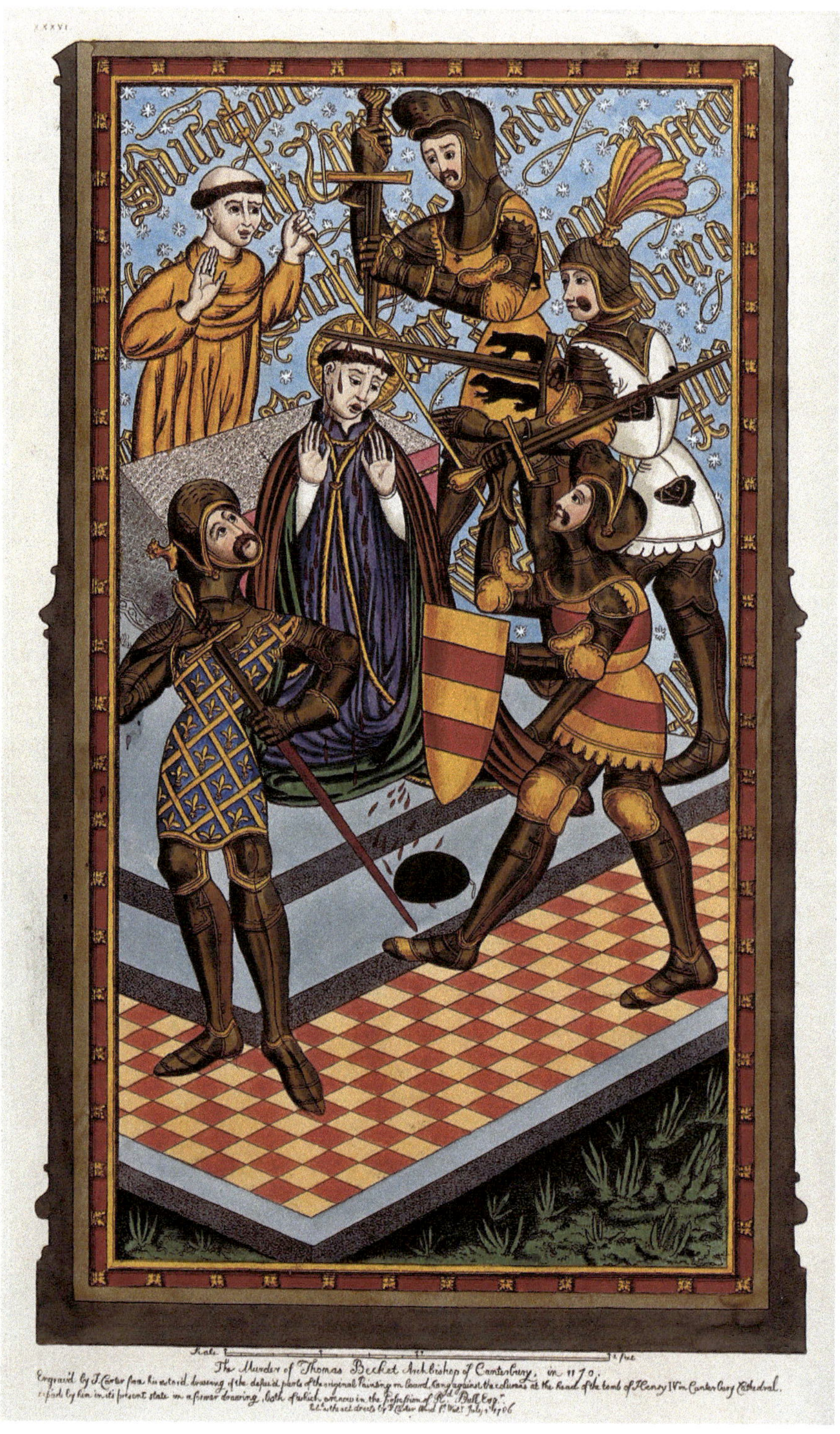

The martyrdom of Saint Thomas of Canterbury, by John Carter, 1786.

After gaining high recognition for this work, which included his account of Becket's life, Alan was appointed as abbot of Tewkesbury in 1186. Nevertheless, while the appointment could be viewed as promotion it was also partly motivated as a way to remove Alan from Canterbury and far away from Henry. Initially, therefore, Alan was disappointed with his move, comparing what he termed 'suffering this punishment of relegation' with Thomas Becket's own exile. However, he soon began to feel at home in Tewkesbury, commenting that he had vacated 'a place of affliction' for 'a garden of delights'. Much admired for his wisdom and intellect at Tewkesbury, Alan was selected to act as papal judge-delegate in two of the most significant cases of the time, concerning the restoration of monks of Coventry, and arbitration in the dispute between Archbishop Geoffrey of York and his canons. One interesting anecdote from his time at Tewkesbury also relates to the advice he gave to the Abbot of Gloucester who planned to send two Welsh monks to bring a lawsuit against Welsh raiders who were marauding monastery-owned lands. Referring back to an incident in Becket's life, which involved the use of trained wolves to deal with a pack of wild ones, Alan opined that the Welsh monks, like Becket's wolves, would end up 'tak[ing] to the life of the woods'. Alan's legacy deserves to be cherished as much as the martyred saint upon whose example he modelled his own life.

The Town Crier

Dating back to medieval times, and even before, town criers were the recognised way of making public proclamations on any subject before the advent of general literacy. Today, while many towns and cities still have criers, either on a paid or voluntary basis, their duties have become ceremonial in nature, focused mainly on contributing to special occasions, and local and charity events.

By the eighteenth century, town criers' duties in Tewkesbury included help with loading and unloading coal barges at the town quay, for which, as a perk, the incumbent routinely received half a hundredweight of coal per barge. Nevertheless, in 1773 the council decided to change the rule, deeming that all official perks should be shared between the crier and one of the Sergeants at Mace. John Pilley, the then crier, objected and, soon, after much wrangling, the decision was revoked.

One of the early incumbents of the post, whose fine portrait can be seen in the upper chamber of the Town Hall, was James Rice. Among the tasks he carried out in 1809 was to serve as the point of contact for a lost colt which had strayed into the local neighbourhood. At other times the role helped to save human lives. In 1868, for example, Henry Newman, then crier, used his handkerchief as a tourniquet around a young butcher's thigh after the unfortunate youth had slipped with knife in hand, injuring himself. Nevertheless, later, in 1873, Newman showed himself in a less favourable light when a case was heard at the Borough Police Court. Newman had satirised Edwin Gay, a carpenter, in a cry designed to oppose Gay's Conservative political views. After Gay retaliated with threatening behaviour Newman had him arrested; but it was Newman who was reprimanded and ordered by the magistrates not to offend again.

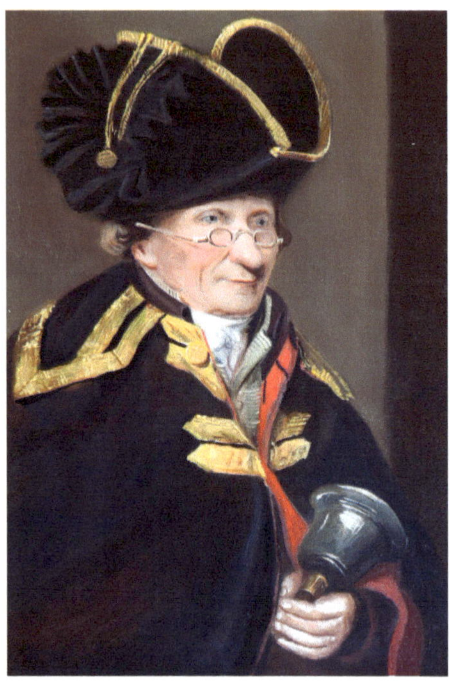

James Rice, Common Crier of Tewkesbury
by British (English) School, *c.* 1820.

Over the years the role has generated much amusement. In April 1887, for example, James Gilchrist, the then incumbent, made the following announcement:

Lost in Station Street for a very long time a watering cart belonging to the ratepayers. Whosoever will find the same and bring it back to Station Street in good working order, and will use it liberally, shall be well rewarded by the ratepayers.

Occasionally though the humour has also strayed into political affairs. One such example occurred in March 1908 when, in an eagerly anticipated contest between the Tories and the Liberals, both aiming to secure victory at the Hastings bye-election – dubbed 'the new Battle of Hastings' – four Liberal-minded Tewkesburians had travelled to the south coast

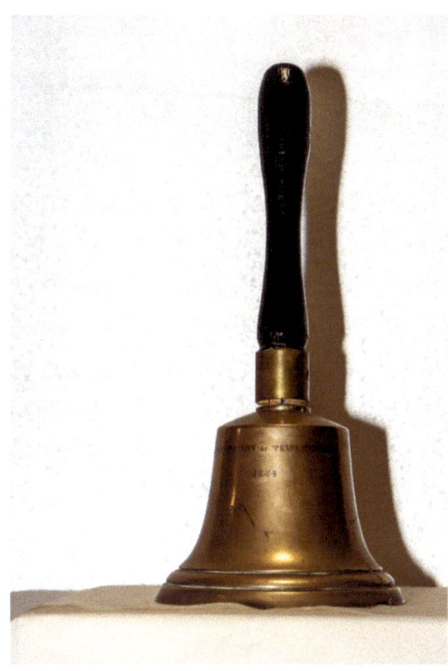

The town crier's bell in Tewkesbury Museum.

to witness the event. Then, on the eve of the election, which ended in a crushing defeat for the Liberals, a Conservative instructed the crier to make the following announcement:

> O'yez, O'yez, O'yez. Missing from this Borough. Four able-bodied men, a retired carpenter, a bricklayer, a bun maker, and a general dealer. Last seen on the London and South-Eastern Railway. All information to be left at the Swan Hotel. God save the King.

Another amusing incident occurred following Tom Green's appointment as town crier in 1928. Debating the issue of a possible replacement hat for him, which, eventually, resulted in a silk hat being chosen, the *Cheltenham Chronicle* reported the town council's discussion as follows:

> Some members thought it should be a silk hat, when others observed that seeing the Crier was a tall man he would not able to stand under the pavement blinds. Others wanted a three-cornered hat, but this was ruled out, as it was stated that such a hat would require a pair of knickers to be in keeping with it ... .

Finally, at times the town crier seems to have acted with overzealous patriotism. In March 1900, for example, during the high emotions stirred up by the Second Boer War, the crier announced that any Boer sympathisers would be taken to the Town Cross and tarred and feathered. The cry stimulated a call to arms from around 200 local youths who paraded through the streets, following the crier. Although they congregated around the house of one suspected sympathiser, nothing more ensued other than loud shouting and, later, the delivery of a pig's head which had been used for target practice.

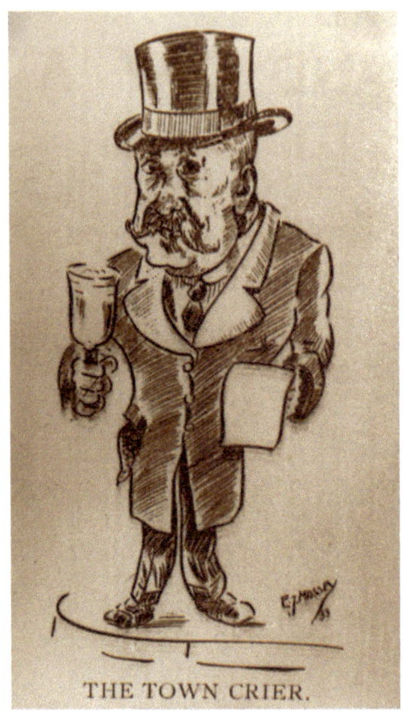

Tom Green, the crier from 1928 to 1938.

Moses Goodere (1752–1838)

Among the town's most respected and well-liked residents was the Worcester-born Quaker Moses Goodere, who lived in the town for nearly fifty years. Initially serving as a glove maker's apprentice in his father's business, thereafter, he rented a large farm near Worcester. Later, in Tewkesbury, his knowledge of agriculture led him, in 1820, for six weeks during the summer, to rent out 192 acres of meadow pasture for cattle and horses to graze on the Ham, using a scale of charges for prospective customers that ranged from 1s per week for weaning calves to 4s for mares and colts. Nevertheless, it was as a confectioner, operating from large premises in Church Street next to the Hop Pole Inn, which made him prosperous. While his shop's frontage measured only 21 feet, his rear premises extended back over 300 feet to the bank of the Avon. In 1786 he married Mary Millard (d. 1822) of Tewkesbury, with whom he had a daughter, Esther. Active in political life as a Conservative, Goodere was also a strict follower of the Society of Friends. Perhaps the most eventful episode in his life, however, occurred in 1792 when he was chosen to give evidence to a House of Commons Committee, commenting:

> That the Parish of Tewkesbury is large and populous, and the Poor thereof exceedingly numerous, and are maintained at a great Expence – That the said Poor might be more effectually relieved and maintained, and at much less Expence, if Powers were given to provide a convenient Place for their Reception, and employ and regulate them in a proper Manner.

Although this led to an Act establishing a House of Industry (now converted into Shephard Mead retirement homes) in 1792–96 to meet these requirements at a southern site on the Gloucester Road, some of the townsfolk vehemently opposed it, even branding

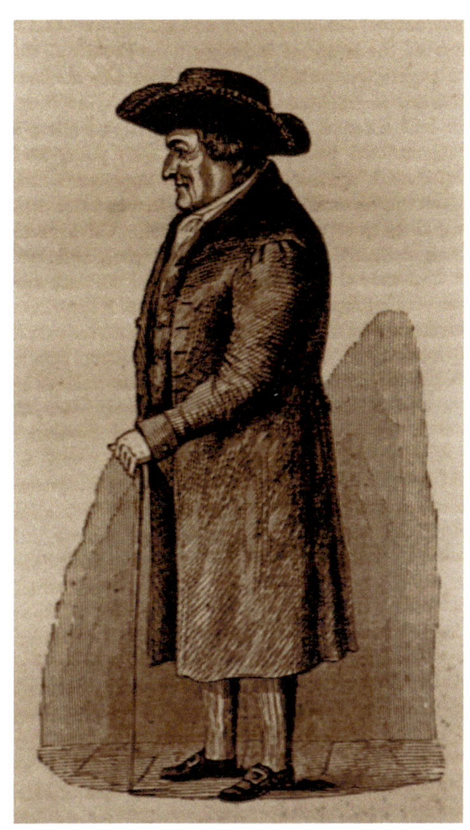

Right: A portrait of Moses Goodere, produced in his eighties.

Below: The House of Industry, now converted into retirement homes.

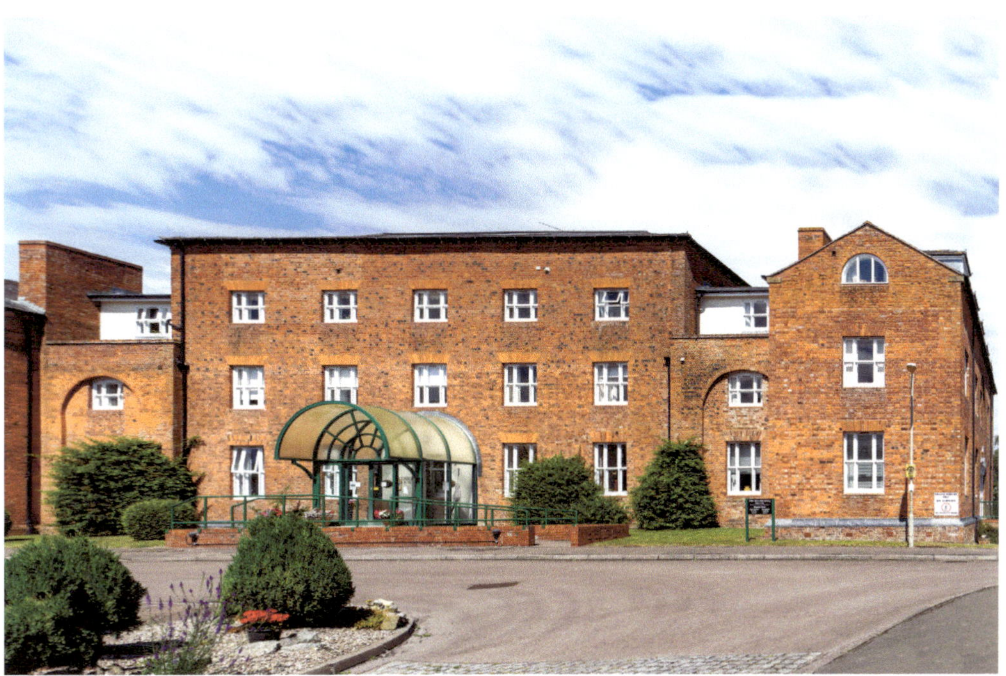

it 'the Bastille'. Goodere was singled out as one of the perceived 'oppressors', on several occasions the windows of his house being smashed by unruly mobs of protesters. Once, when the crowd was intent on destroying his property, the magistrates had to intervene through reading the Riot Act. In his obituary *The Tewkesbury Register* described Goodere as being 'truly honest and conscientious in all the relations of life' while also appearing slightly eccentric, greeting everyone he met with a fond but peculiar salutation. High regard for Goodere continued for many years to come. In 1870, for example, more than thirty years after his death, *The Register* reported that Goodere's spirit was summoned at a Local Board of Health meeting when the poor state of the town's roads was being discussed. Debating the necessary requirements for building a good road, one official suggested that Mr Goodere's well-known practice to ensure that the stones used were of a consistently small but uniform size could be used. However, given that this involved breaking up the stone sufficiently so that each one would fit in one's mouth without inconvenience, this was not without its inherent danger: on one occasion, it was said, Goodere nearly choked to death when one of the stones became lodged in his throat!

Edmund Rudge (*c.* 1759–1843)

Among Tewkesbury's most eccentric characters was the miserly tanner Edmund Rudge, dubbed the 'Jemmy Wood of Tewkesbury' after the famous Gloucester miser. When he died at the age of eighty-four he had amassed a fortune of around £145,000, which equates

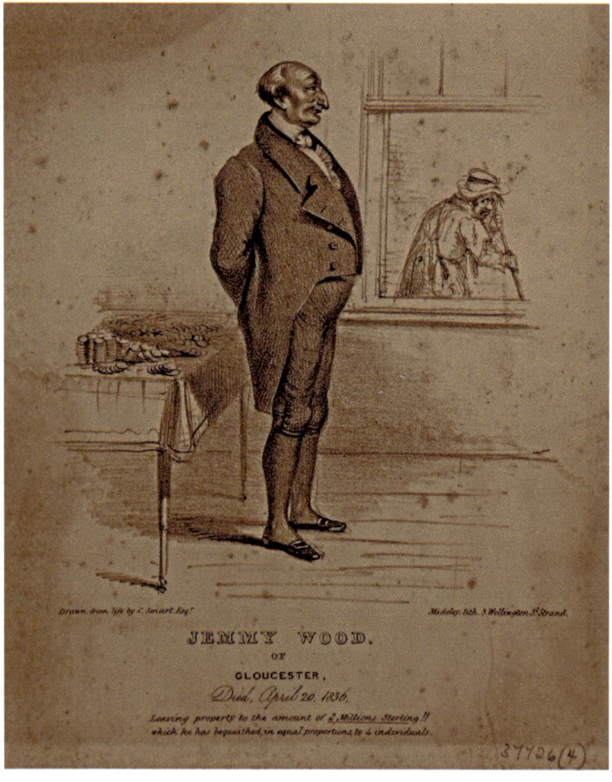

Jemmy Wood, whose portrait Rudge kept in his kitchen.

to over £20 million today. While he had worked tirelessly throughout his life, denying himself even the most basic of comforts, he lived in what the *Gloucester Journal* described as 'a mean and filthy habitation and neighbourhood' in St Mary's Lane. Unmarried and without domestic help, he scrimped and saved wherever possible. When purchasing skins at Gloucester docks, for example, he never used the services of a porter, relying instead on using his own wheelbarrow, which necessitated making several journeys. Once, when the opportunity arose to purchase hides at Cork at bargain prices, he walked around 135 miles to Milford Haven, from where he worked his passage to Ireland. Then, after negotiating favourable freight charges for the return journey he included himself as part of the freight deal, the total cost of his entire trip not exceeding 7*s*.

Given Rudge's opulence he was often a target for theft. One Saturday evening in January 1822, for example, when he was walking back from Gloucester market, he was assaulted near Southwick Park by someone wielding a heavy bludgeon. Despite suffering a fractured skull and additional head injuries from the subsequent struggle, he held off the assailant until the latter was scared off by another traveller. While 'more timid souls', the *Gloucester Journal* claimed, would have required lengthy recuperation and the services of a phlebotomist or apothecary, Rudge simply walked home, applied some turpentine to his wounds, and bandaged his head with his handkerchief. Then, before dawn on Monday, he was hard at work, up to his middle in one of his tan pits, as if nothing had happened.

DID YOU KNOW?
The geologist and Antarctic explorer Sir Raymond Edward Priestley (1886–1974) was born in Tewkesbury and attended the grammar school at a time when his father was headmaster. Priestley was the geologist on Shackleton's *Nimrod* Expedition (1907–09) and was part of the advance team that laid food and fuel depots for the 1909 attempt to reach the South Pole. He was also a member of Captain Scott's ill-fated *Terra Nova* Expedition (1910–13) but not involved in the tragic ending. He later became Vice-Chancellor of Birmingham and Melbourne universities. He revisited the Antarctic in 1946 with Prince Philip. He was knighted by the Queen.

Rudge seems to have been inspired by Jemmy Wood, who, incidentally, once hitched a lift in the back of a hearse when travelling from Tewkesbury to Gloucester rather than pay for a fare, given that Rudge kept Wood's portrait in his kitchen. Yet, despite this, Rudge was perhaps a more balanced character than many believed. It was known, for instance, that he kept beer, and even wine, in the house, occasionally offering these to visitors. Furthermore, he lent financial support to close relatives who got into difficulty and, for some time, considered funding almshouses for the poor. The extent to which he was a true miser, therefore, is a secret he took with him to his family's grave, still visible in the abbey churchyard.

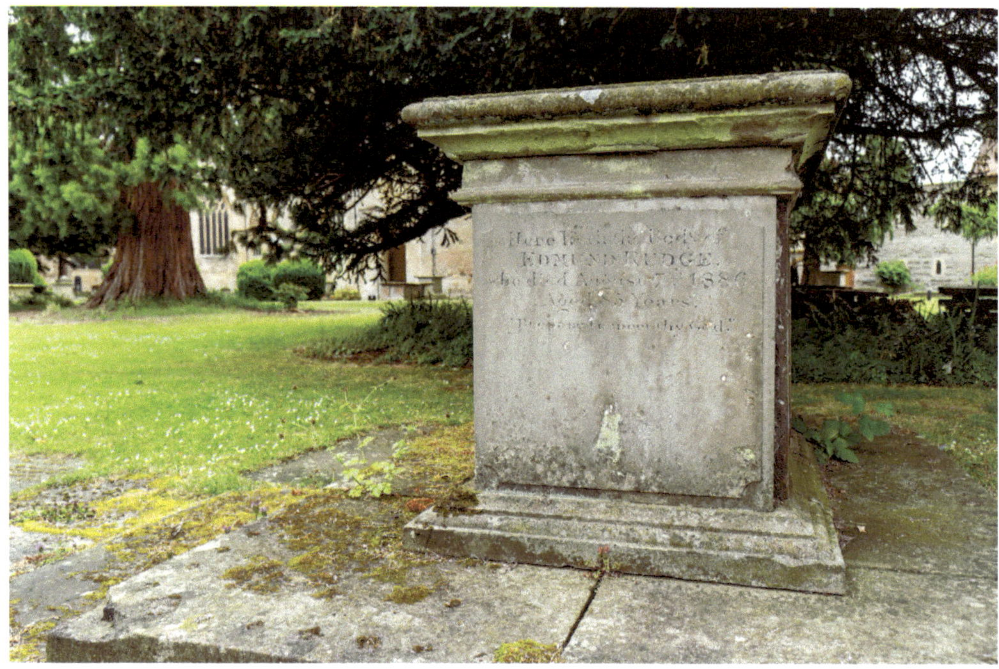

The raised tomb of Edmund Rudge.

William Sandilands (*c.* 1778–1867)

Among the town's most celebrated sons, albeit with some mystery surrounding his life, is William Sandilands, in whose memory a plaque may be found inside Holy Trinity Church. Identified as William Saunders when he signed up to serve on HMS *Victory*, the Able Seaman came to prominence after helping to carry Admiral Nelson's wounded body to the cockpit of the *Victory* at the Battle of Trafalgar (1805). It seems possible that he omitted the 'lands' from his name because of its potential association with the naval rank of 'landsman', which refers to a seaman with less than a year's experience at sea. His story is probably accurately told by the Revd Francis John Scott in the latter's account published in *Notes and Queries* in 1867. As Incumbent of Holy Trinity Church in 1849–79 and grandson of Nelson's secretary, who had been shot on-board the *Victory* prior to Nelson, Scott met Sandilands on a number of occasions, even witnessing his quarterdeck saying that Scott's writings were too 'racy' for publication in the journal. He also reported how, on the day of the battle, Sandilands had stashed away his £90 savings in his neckerchief so that, if he were killed, they would be lost at sea, along with himself, rather than end up in officers' hands. Sandilands recounted as well how he was called upon to leave his gun position three times: firstly, to help lash another ship to the *Victory's* rigging; then to carry the injured Lieutenant Rivers, who lost a leg; and, finally, to help carry the dying Nelson who, he said, seemed pleased after Sandilands reported back to him from Captain Hardy the number of strikes made by the French and Spanish navies. Following the outpouring of national grief the American neoclassicist Benjamin West (1738–1820) was among several artists who commemorated Nelson's death on canvas.

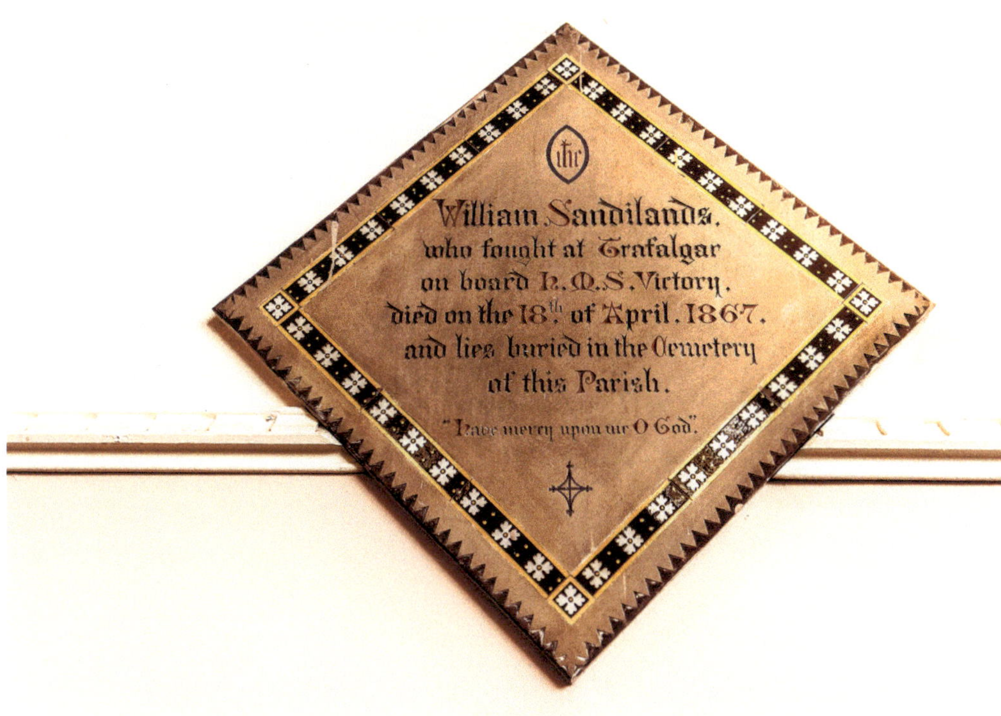

Commemorative plaque of William Sandilands, Holy Trinity Church.

To ensure accurate representation of the event around thirty of the survivors, including, in early 1806, William Saunders, visited West's studio to have their sketches made. The final work portrayed Saunders kneeling in front of Nelson, laying a captured Spanish flag (possibly from the *Santissima Trinidad*) at the admiral's feet.

Later, Sandilands came to national attention following publication of a letter in *The Times* on 25 September 1861, which drew attention to the fact that at the age of eighty-three he was living as a lodger in poor conditions in Avonside, specifically South Quay Road, in the same plot as No. 33 High Street today. While he received a £5 annual allowance from the Dowager Countess Nelson, the value of this was reduced from his income by the local Poor Law Guardians, 'thus leaving this old man to exist upon 3s. 6d. per week, occasionally increased by donations from kind friends in Tewkesbury!' Such a situation, it was suggested, would never have arisen in France where 'he would be decorated, honoured, cared for, and nursed as a child of the State...'. However, following an appeal, Holy Trinity Church and donors from wider afield provided a substantial donation to help to guarantee his pension for the remaining years of his life. Although research by Sam Eedle in 2005 and 2006 highlighted potentially inconclusive evidence about Sandilands' case, including the mystery of not using his real name and the possibility of him being a fraudster, the account provided by the Revd Scott, which includes confirmation that Sandilands still owned his naval uniform and Trafalgar medal, together with Eedle's latest research, published in 2013, proved Sandilands' authenticity beyond doubt.

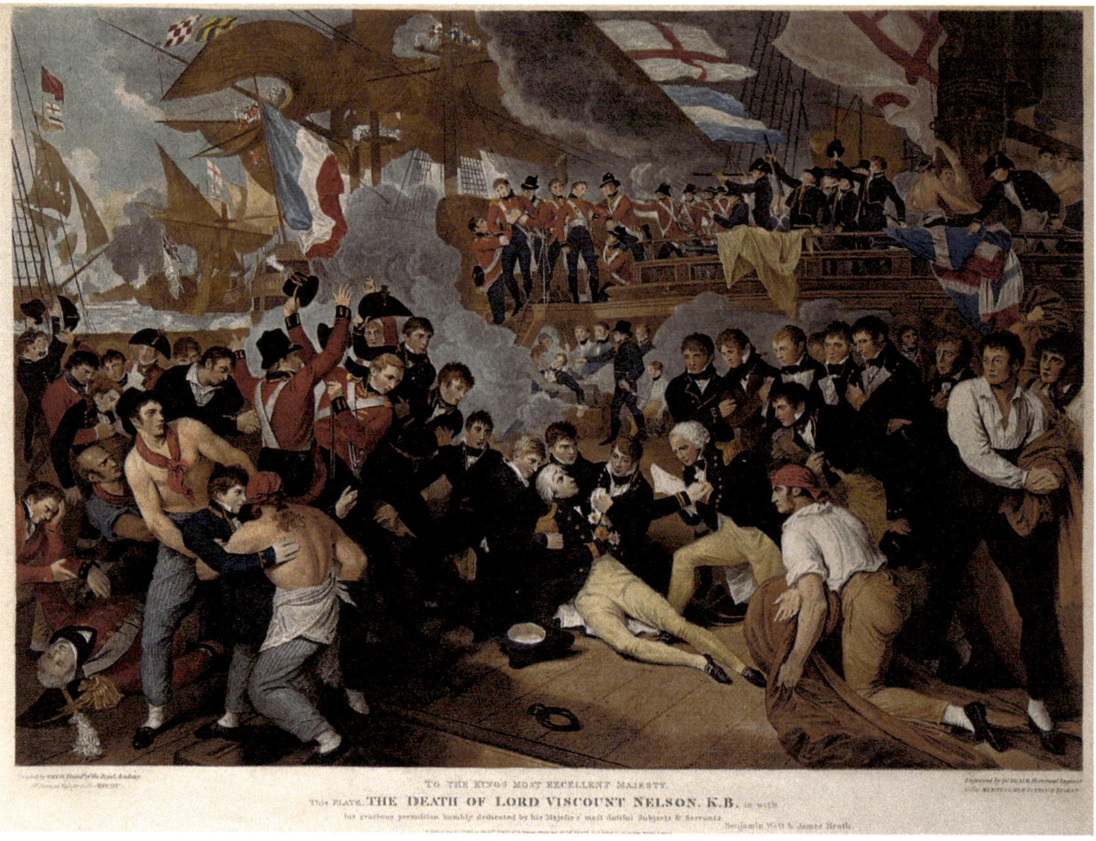

The death of Lord Nelson, by J. Heath, 1811, after B. West.

Victoria Woodhull (1838–1927)

Among the most unusual and remarkable women associated with Tewkesbury is Victoria Woodhull (née Claflin), later Victoria Woodhull-Martin. In 1871 she was the first woman to be heard by the Judiciary Committee of Congress. As a result she became a candidate for presidency of the United States, and became the most popular speaker and lecturer in America. More controversially she had been married twice, firstly to Dr Woodhull, by whom she had two children – a son and daughter, Zula – and, following his death, she married James Blood. In her public speaking period, she expressed controversial opinions on taboo subjects, such as short skirts, spiritualism, vegetarianism, sex education, free love, and prostitution. She had also formed a realtionship with the widowed and rich Cornelius Vanderbilt who allegedly improved her financial acumen and helped fund her political aspirations. It is also thought that she was so feared as a candidate that when she attempted to file her presidential application she was put in prison charged with publishing defamatory articles.

After she retired from her public life because of her health, she then visited Europe and met her third husband whilst lecturing in London in 1877. She married John Biddulph Martin, a banker and part of the Overbury Martin family, in 1880. He died in 1897 and, a few

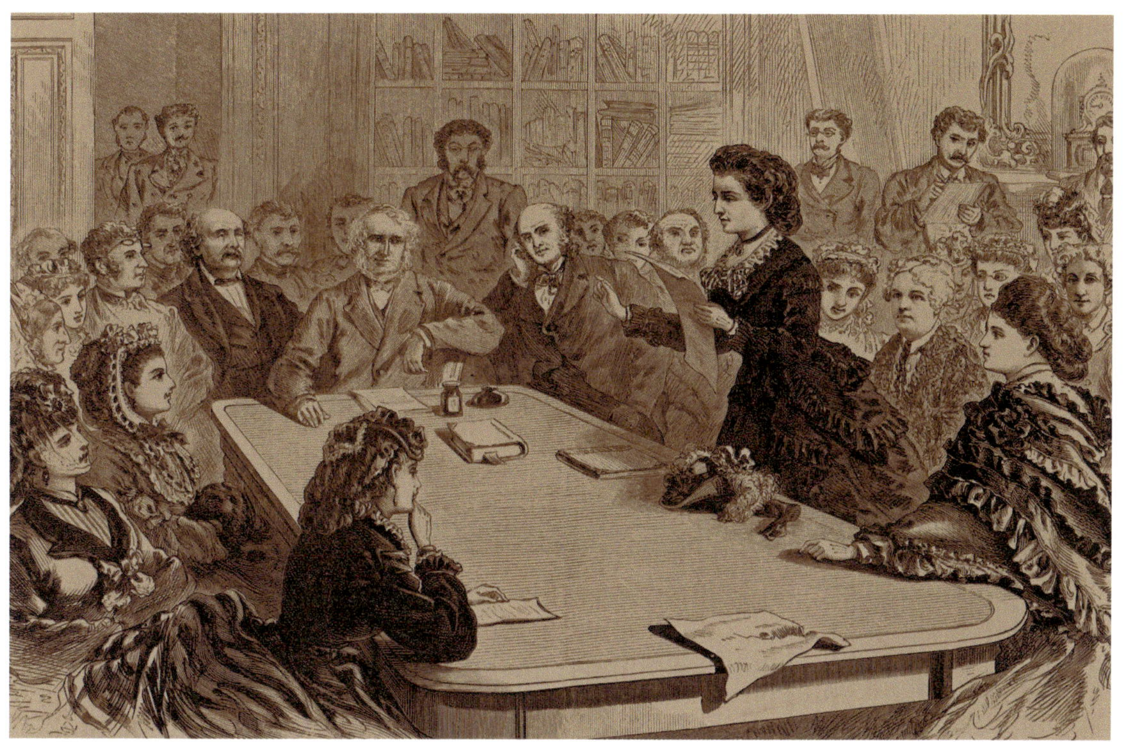

Victoria Woodhull addressing the US House of Representatives Judiciary Committee, 1871.

years afterwards, she retired to Norton Park where she became renowned as the beneficent Lady of the Manor. She could still be controversial advocating many things, which we now take for granted, such as an eight-hour working day and social welfare programmes. Because of her work in the village, she was a popular figure in and around Tewkesbury: according to the *Tewkesbury Reporter* her Talbot-Darraacq was seen almost daily in the town carrying 'delicacies and good cheer for sick and needy, purchased and distributed by her own hand.' In 1925 her philanthropy even extended to improving the local roads when she funded the construction of a 1,100-yard-long road up Bredon Hill, using only local labour.

She died in 1927 leaving much of her fortune to her unmarried daughter, Zula, and in 1941 her legacy enabled the Abbey Lawn Trustees to purchase the late medieval cottages at Nos 34–39 Church Street, together with 2 acres of land to the east of the abbey to maintain uninterrupted views from Gloucester Road. This generous donation was on condition that a memorial tablet to her mother should be sited inside the abbey. Erected in 1943, it is located in the Chapel of St Faith, the tablet, decorated with two flags, serving as a reminder to what this remarkable woman achieved in relation to improving Anglo-American friendship.

In 2000, it was reported in the local press that a film biography was in preparation, starring Nicole Kidman and Tom Cruise. As it surely would have focused on the controversial American period of her life, it is perhaps good for her reputation that the film did not materialise.

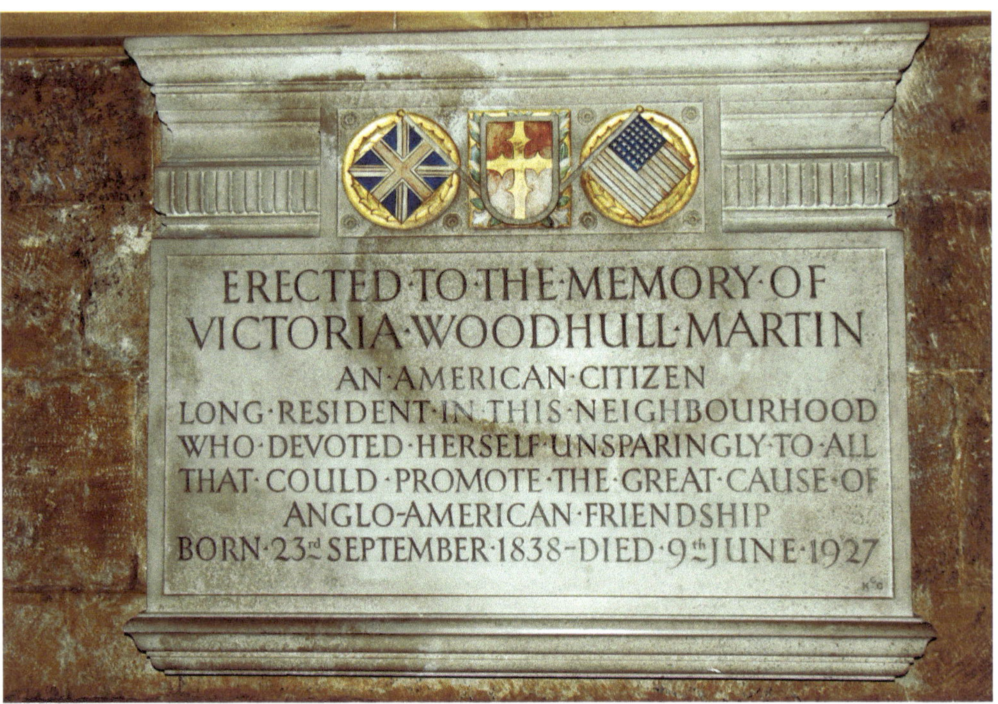

The memorial plaque at Tewkesbury Abbey.

DID YOU KNOW?

The comedian Eric Morecambe (1926–84) gave his last performance at the Roses Theatre. Tragically, on 27 May 1984, after Morecambe's final curtain call, he collapsed at the back of the stage, where he suffered a heart attack from which he never recovered. Dr Andrew Crowther responded as a 'doctor in the house' but he needed to be taken to Cheltenham Hospital where he had a further fatal heart attack in the early hours of the next morning. Later as a tribute to the comedian, the Roses Theatre named its committee room after him.

3. Crime and Punishment

Among the early crimes committed against Tewkesburians were cases of pillaging and murder by marauders from the Forest of Dean, who attacked boats on the River Severn travelling from Tewkesbury to Bristol. In 1429 the townspeople complained about this piracy to King Henry VI, which led, the following year, to the passing of an Act protecting the boatmen along the King's Water Highway. While a gaol existed in Barton Street, possibly in the building now occupied by the museum, from at least 1547 it was the charter issued to Tewkesbury by Elizabeth I in 1574, which officially confirmed the town bailiff's rights to provide a prison and hold courts. Thereafter, Tewkesbury came under scrutiny to ensure compliance. Indeed, when the Queen's Justices inspected the gaol in 1582 they were dissatisfied and ordered a new gaol to be commissioned which would also serve half of the county. This was achieved through converting the abbey's bell tower, whose site is now occupied by the Abbey Tea Rooms in Church Street. Nevertheless, how suitable the building was for its new purpose remains doubtful. James Bennett described 'large rents or fissures on the [building's] west side', probably caused by vibrations of the bells, which made it uncomfortable and insecure.

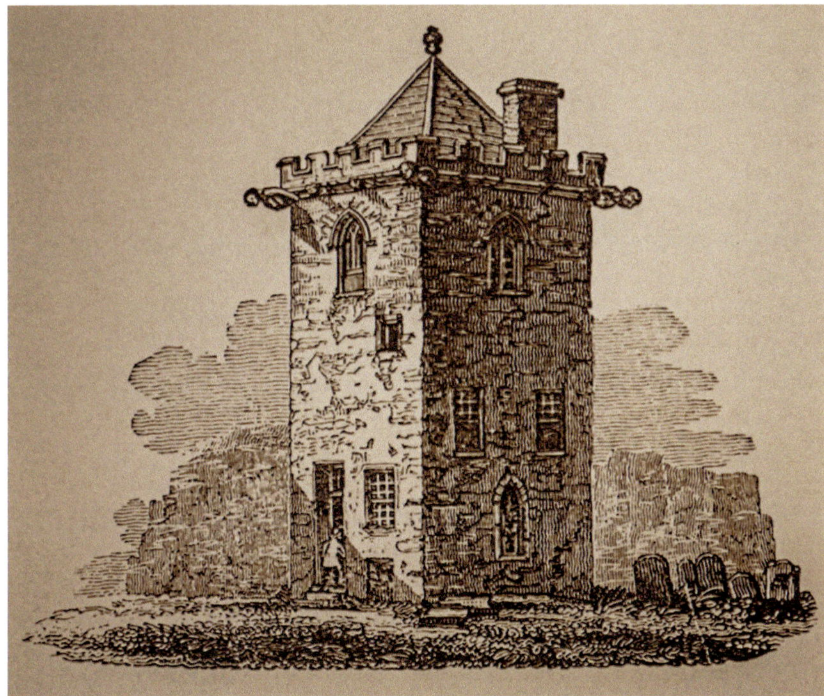

The abbey bell tower, used as the town's gaol from the sixteenth century.

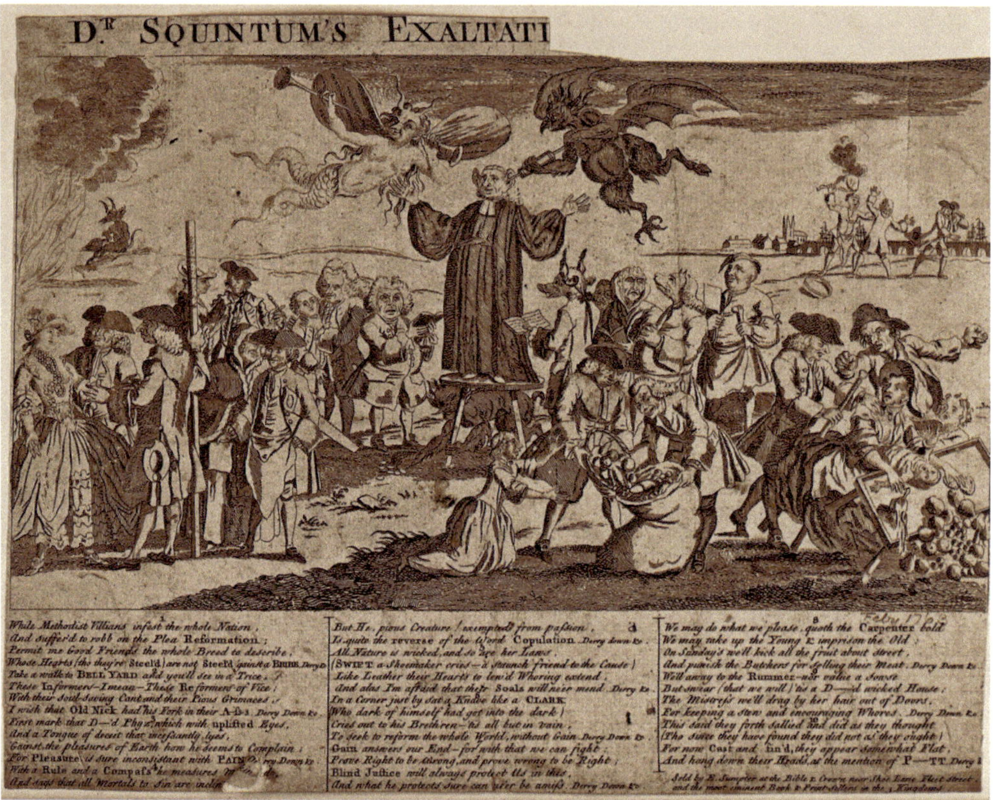

George Whitefield preaching to a crowd of supporters, 1763.

Under the provisions of the royal charter, while the duty of keeping the peace rested on the shoulders of the bailiffs, magistrates and constables, at times, the perceived threat of large gatherings unduly alarmed the bailiffs. In July 1739, for example, when the Gloucester-born cleric George Whitefield (1714–70) visited the town, intending to preach the gospel, the bailiff sent four constables to arrest or frighten him away. Nevertheless, after a lawyer friend of Whitefield challenged them to produce a valid warrant the constables were sent away, leaving Whitefield to preach to a crowd of around 2,500. A few days later, he preached again in a field by the town, this time to a 6,000-strong crowd, without any constables accosting him.

Crossroads Burials

Among the town's most atrocious murders occurring around the end of the eighteenth century were the (coincidental) cases of two carpenters: both sentenced to be hanged at Gloucester Gaol, they ended up committing suicide and were later buried at crossroads in Tewkesbury. While mystery still surrounds this practice, which began from at least medieval times and continued until the passing of the Burial of Suicide Act of 1823, possible theories include that crossroads were once considered as unearthly places or thought to either provide a religious symbol for the deceased or confuse their spirit about which path to take.

The first case concerned twenty-six-year-old William Birt, who, after making his girlfriend Sarah Powell pregnant – a servant in a respectable household – gave her some poison to induce an abortion. Then, having convinced her that he had swallowed twice the amount of the powder and it would only do her good, she suffered immediate sickness and died eleven days later. After initially being held at Tewkesbury Gaol, Birt was sent to trial at the Gloucestershire Assizes in August 1791. Such was the speculation in Tewkesbury about Birt's guilt that a vagrant was committed to Tewkesbury gaol after circulating handbills which prejudged the verdict. Nevertheless, Birt was found guilty of murder, rather than manslaughter, and condemned to death. The judge drew on the legal

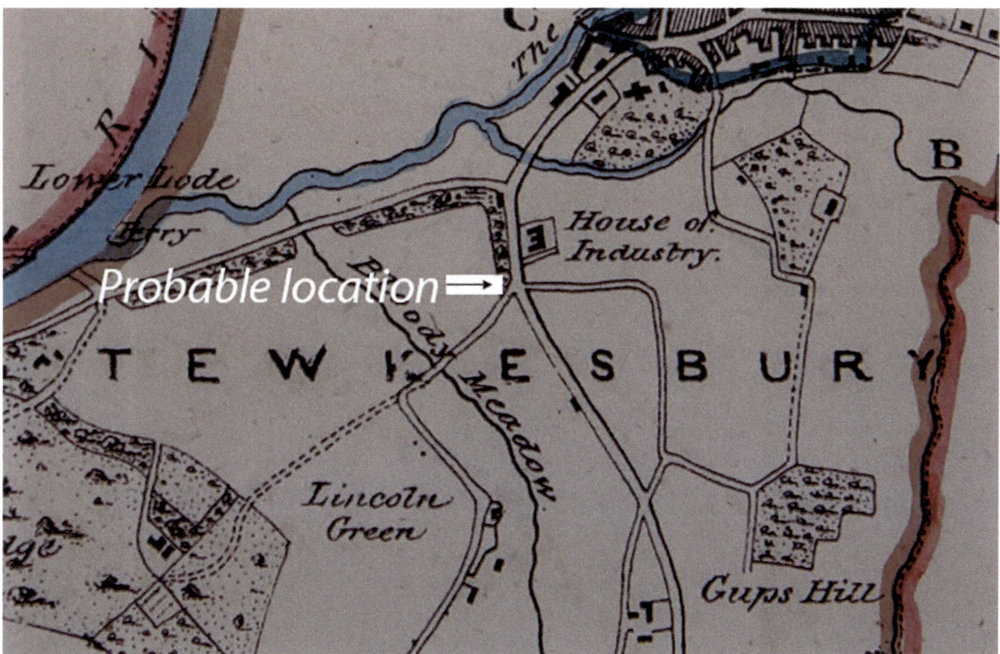

Probable site of the burial, shown on an 1835 map.

principle that 'where Death ensues in consequence of an illegal Act, Malice is implied, and the offence, with its consequences, is deemed Murder'. Birt would have become the first person to be executed on the gatehouse roof of the new gaol, which opened during the summer, had he not used his bed sheet to hang himself. Significantly, a verdict of *felo de se* (literally 'felon of him/herself'), or suicide, from the coroner's inquest meant that, in accordance with prevailing practice, the body would be buried at a crossroads, possibly with a stake through the heart, and without any Christian ceremony. In Birt's case the probable site chosen, as identified through research by Jill Evans, was the intersection that once existed near the workhouse (now Shephard Mead), comprising Gloucester Road, the small lane leading to the cemetery, and Lincoln Green Lane, which previously joined the latter when it was slightly more aligned to the north.

The second case related to John Young, from Longdon, who murdered his wife on the Ham on 15 February 1800 while returning home from Tewkesbury market. After her body was discovered in the Severn on 29 March, with her hands tied and a sack over her head, it was subsequently proven that she was heavily pregnant. Although Young was sent to Gloucester Gaol, he was found in his cell on the morning of his trial on 1 August, hanging by a handkerchief. According to James Bennett he was then 'buried in the cross-way at the bottom of Pagett's lane, near the river, at the Mythe'.

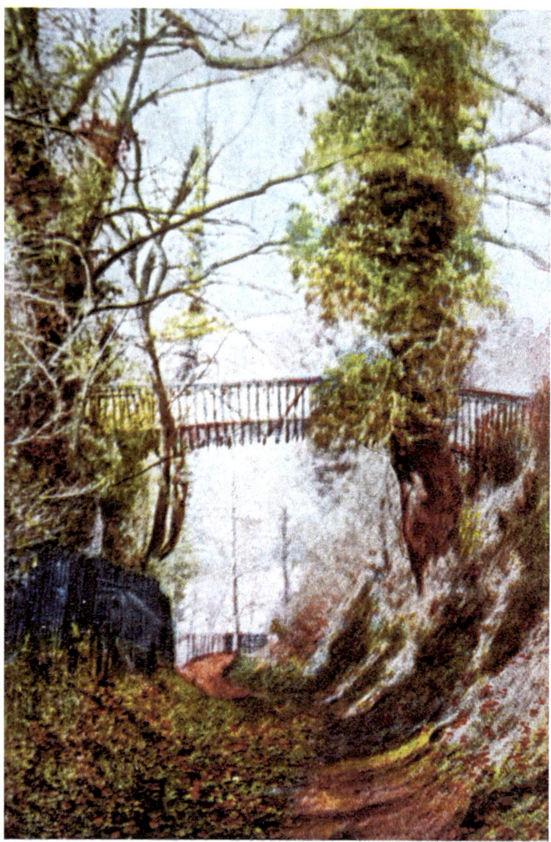

Paget's Lane, near where Young was buried.

Policing and Prison Reform

At the beginning of the nineteenth century, various improvements were made to the town's policing. In 1812, the number of constables was increased from four to six. However, by the autumn of 1831, when Tewkesbury faced potential rioting from striking stocking makers demanding higher wages, a troop of the 14th Light Dragoons was sent from Gloucester to provide reinforcements. Additional precautions were taken to swear in around 450 special constables, which led to the almost universal absence of crime within the town at a time when most of the country was experiencing heightened tension. Nevertheless, the subsequent establishment of an organised police force under the Municipal Corporation Act of 1835 caused some disquiet. According to Bennett this was fuelled by a significant 'degree of jealousy in the minds of the uninformed and the lawless', which resulted in a serious disturbance on 28 June 1836. Following the conviction of five men who assaulted the police, the populace showed their displeasure by stoning and hurling other missiles at the body of police officers and special constables, which escorted the offenders to the borough gaol. Eventually, however, following the identification and arrest of further offenders, the police received the community's support. In 1839 the Town Hall, originally built in the High Street in 1788, was enlarged to accommodate a police station with cells.

By 1811, following increased national demands for prison reform, Tewkesbury found itself under increasing pressure to improve the conditions of its gaol. A committee was formed which recommended the replacement of the old bell tower with a new purpose-built gaol. After the passing of the Tewkesbury Gaol Act 1813, a new brick building in Bredon Road, now partly occupied by a dental surgery, was opened in December 1816.

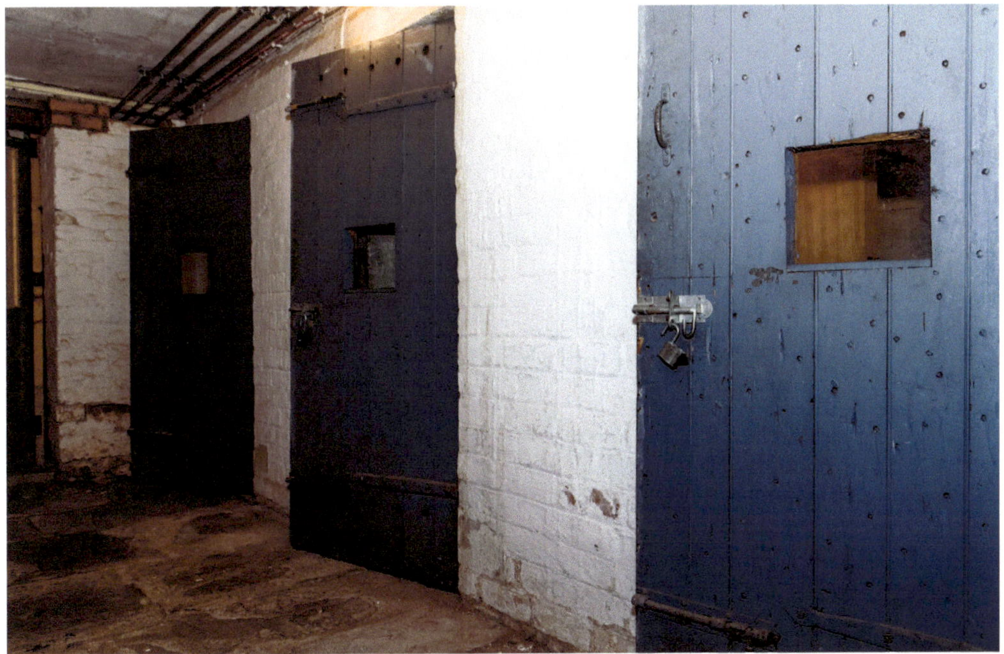

Disused prison cells in the basement of the Town Hall building.

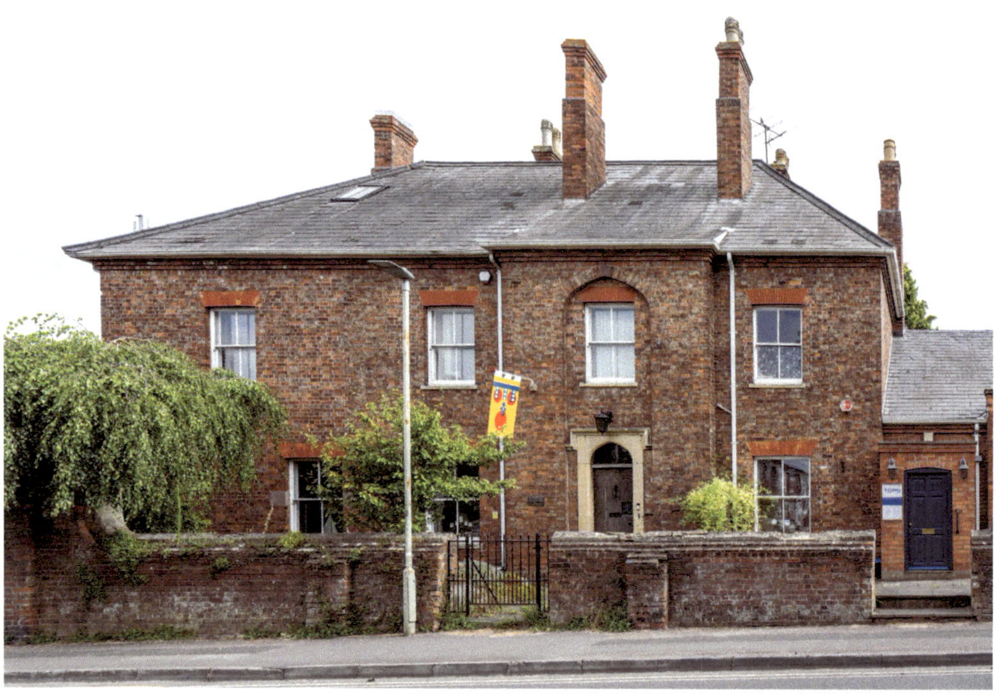

The old gaol and police station, Bredon Road.

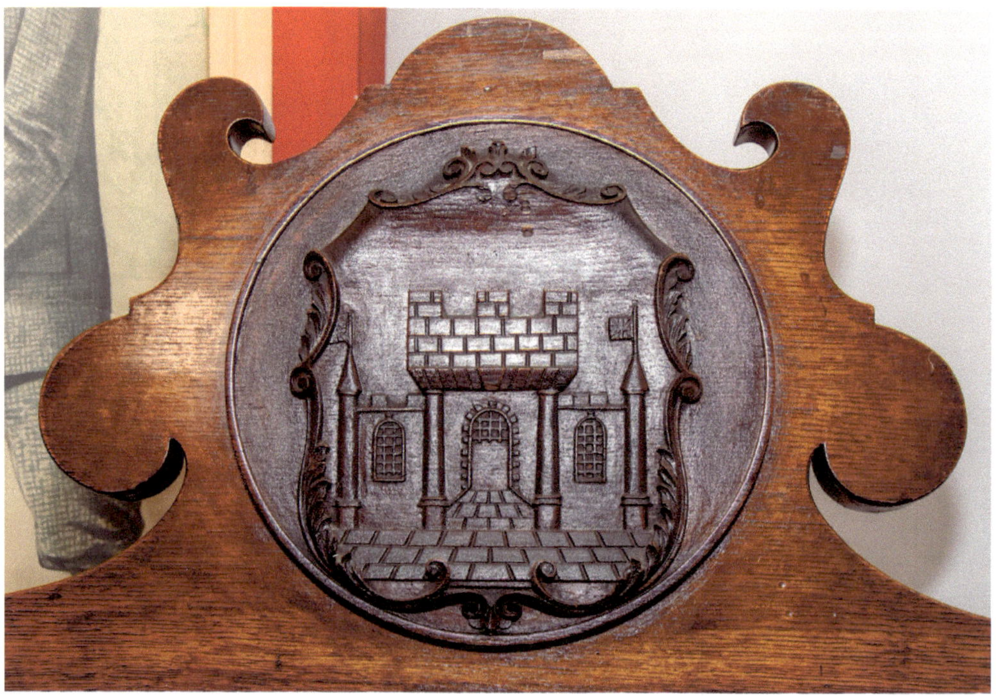

Detail from the magistrates' chair in Tewkesbury Museum.

Nevertheless, further enlargement and security improvements soon followed, partly necessitated by the ease with which, in April 1817, sixteen-year-old Thomas Macklow escaped after his imprisonment for stealing money from the British School in Barton Road (now Elizabeth Wyatt House). Despite these improvements conditions remained harsh for the prisoners. The 1817 accounts, for example, show that 90 per cent of food expenditure was spent on bread, with only 5 per cent on meat. By 1828, a treadmill had been purchased, forcing the inmates to undertake the hard labour of grinding corn. Ten years later, questions were raised about the regime imposed by the gaoler following attacks made by his fierce dog, and an investigating committee of 1840 instructed that one of the gaol's punishment rooms, nicknamed 'the Black Hole', be converted into a standard cell. Despite taking this corrective action, the Borough Council still needed to make further improvements. To deal with the additional burden on ratepayers, the council made the novel proposal of paying for its prisoners to be transferred to the county gaol in Gloucester and paying for their board. However, the Borough Council's initial proposed fee of *2s 6d* per prisoner per day proved unattractive. Further negotiation ensued until a charge of *2s* was agreed, with an additional charge of *1d* per mile agreed with the railway company for transporting the prisoners. Following the scheme's implementation Tewkesbury's gaol closed and, from 1855 to 1966, the building reused as its police headquarters. Thenceforward, a new purpose-built police station in Barton Street was utilised and then, from 2012, transferred to the new Borough Council offices in Gloucester Road.

Extract from the prison's accounts, 1822.

The Names of Prisoners remaining in the Tewkesbury Borough Gaol 29 September 1853

Entry	Names	Age	Read or write	Crimes	Religion	Remarks
6 May 1853	James Barnfoot	21	Write	Felony	Church of England	At the Quarter Sessions 8 July 1853 2 Calendar Months
13 May 1853	Henry Arnott	26	R. Imp	Felony	— Do —	At the Quarter Sessions 8 July 1853 7 Years Transportation
13 May 1853	Frederick Joynes	26	R. Imp W. Imp	Felony	— Do —	At the Quarter Sessions 8 July 1853 6 Calendar Months
9 June 1853	Thomas Partridge	19	R. Imp W. Imp	Felony	— Do —	At the Quarter Sessions 8 July 1853 6 Calendar Months
5 September 1853	John Shakespeare	55	Read & W. Imp	unlawfully assaulting with Intent	— Do —	Waiting Trial at the Sessions in October 6 Calendar Months

Prisoners admitted since 29 September 1853

Entry	Names	Age	Read or write	Crimes	Religion	Remarks
30 September 1853	William Beatty	9	R. Imp W. Imp	unlawfully stealing Apples	Church of England	7 Days Common Gaol
25 November 1853	George Hathaway	49	— Do —	unlawfully assaulting	Do	2 Months Common Gaol
23 November 1853	Charles Turner	19	R. Imp W. Imp	unlawfully assaulting	— Do —	3 Months Common Gaol and to find sureties to keep the Peace for 6 months
29 November 1853	Thomas White	55	R. Wri W. Wri	Charged with Vagrancy	— Do —	3 Months House of correction Hard Labour
5 December 1853	Hannah Lucas	15	— Do —	Felony	Wesleyan	1 Calendar Month House of correction Hard Labour

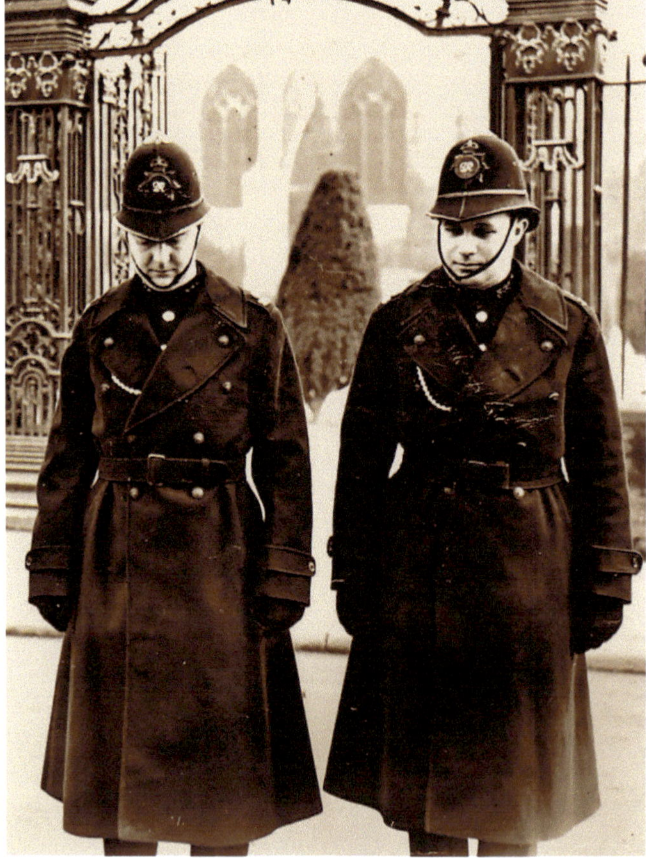

Above: List of prisoners and their crimes, 1853.

Left: Police constables outside Tewkesbury Abbey during George V's commemorative funeral service, 1953.

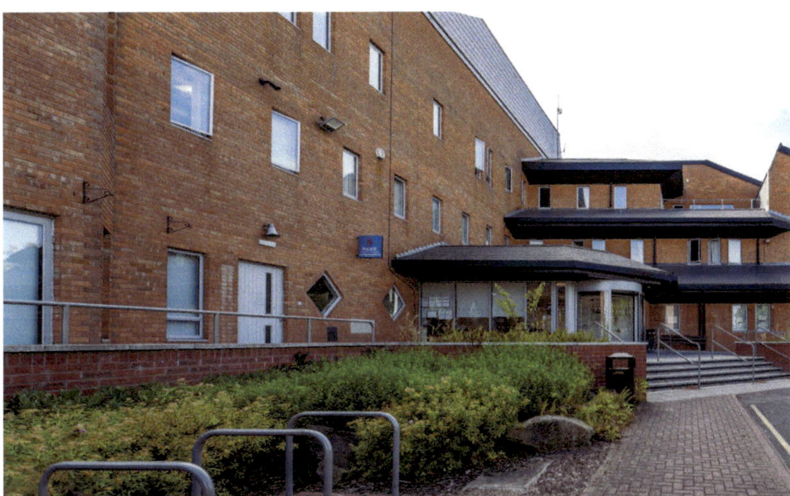

The current
police station.

The Whip Hand

At times Tewkesburians have attempted to take the law into their own hands to mete out punishment. One case concerned Thomas Scott, landlord of the Black Bear Inn, who, together with Nathaniel Chandler, a maltster at Tewkesbury, travelled in a gig to Cheltenham on 11 February 1840. After purchasing a heavy hunting crop with a brass hammer at the butt end, they visited the work premises of Thomas Shenton, the printer and publisher of a weekly satirical newspaper called *Gloucestershire Paul Pry or the Quizzical Gazette*, which carried scurrilous articles full of base scandal and inuendo. Scott then approached Shenton, threatening to give him a good thrashing unless he handed over a letter showing the authorship of various articles printed in the newspaper concerning his wife. Refusing to do this, both Shenton and a solicitor, who happened to be present and tried to intervene in vain, received a brutal beating from Scott, while Chandler kept watch at the door. Shenton's head was badly bruised by the butt end of the crop, and his body received lashes from the whip end, while the solicitor Gregory Tomkins received a blow in the mouth, which severely cut his lip.

DID YOU KNOW?
Certain members of the Codrington family used bribery as part of their strategy for influencing parliamentary elections. Sir William Codrington, the town's MP from 1761 to 1792, who owned plantations in Antigua and was keen to lobby against the abolition of slavery in Parliament, bought up around 150 properties in the town so that he could temporarily transfer their ownership at election time to his tenants and other trusted parties to secure their votes. He also donated the magnificent Town Hall building. In 1798, his nephew and heir Sir Christopher Bethel-Codrington gifted half a guinea each to 115 electors.

During the trial at the Gloucestershire summer assizes, while evidence of the potentially libellous articles, which provoked the attack, was not presented, Shenton maintained that these did not refer to Scott's wife. Despite this, Shenton ceased publication of the newspaper around a week after the attack. Ironically, a caricature by the artist William Heath (1794–1840), who published under the pseudonym Paul Pry (the name of an inquisitive character in a popular comedy by John Poole), once portrayed a printing press with 'the whip hand'. In this case, however, as Shenton discovered to his cost, it was the printing press that received both ends of the whip. While Scott was ordered to pay £5 in damages, Tewkesburians decided to defray the costs through subscription, such was their approval of the punishment inflicted on Shenton.

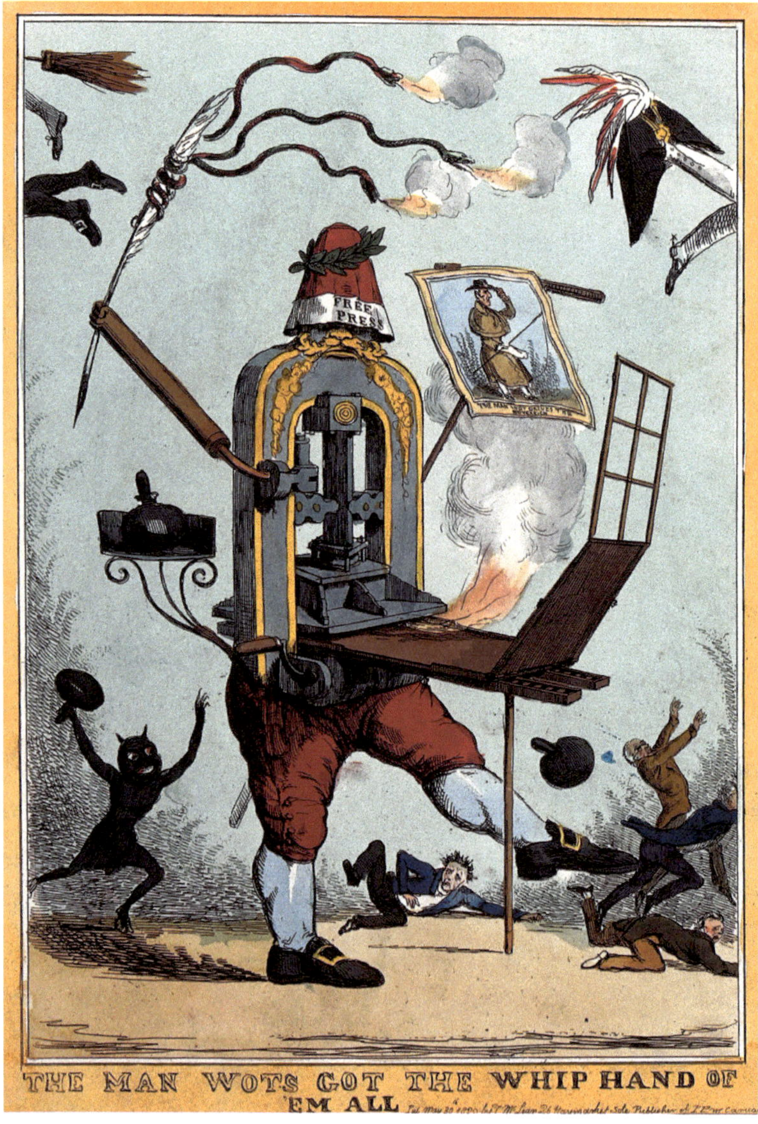

Coloured etching by Paul Pry. (William Heath)

Stealing from the Poor

One of the most despicable crimes recorded during the late Victorian period was the case of a respectable-looking thirty-four-year-old man called Samuel Horton who, after entering Tewkesbury Abbey on 23 April 1896 but declining to sign the visitors' book, was seen by the assistant verger stealing money from St Mary's Guild offertory box. After following Horton to the Hop Pole Royal Hotel, the assistant verger then informed a police constable about the incident. PC Kenny, at that time on duty in the High Street, rushed to the hotel only to see Horton mount his bicycle and escape in the direction of Gloucester. Kenny then took charge of a horse and trap and followed Horton in hot pursuit but only managed to catch up with him, 6 miles further on, at Coombe Hill. An exciting chase followed as Horton tried to dodge Kenny by doubling back to Tewkesbury, but the brave officer leapt from the cart and ran after him. By chance, a Tewkesbury councillor, C. C. Moore, the father of the author John Moore, was also riding his bicycle towards Gloucester and, realising what was happening, helped to delay Horton until Kenny could arrive. A desperate struggle ensued, with Horton trying to use his bicycle spanner as a weapon, but eventually Kenny succeeded in handcuffing him. At the trial, it emerged that Horton had £2 1s 4d in his possession. Moreover, he had committed a spate of similar crimes in churches across the Midlands. As Horton was sentenced to three years' penal servitude, the *Recorder* observed said that he could not conceive 'a more despicable and dirty, mean

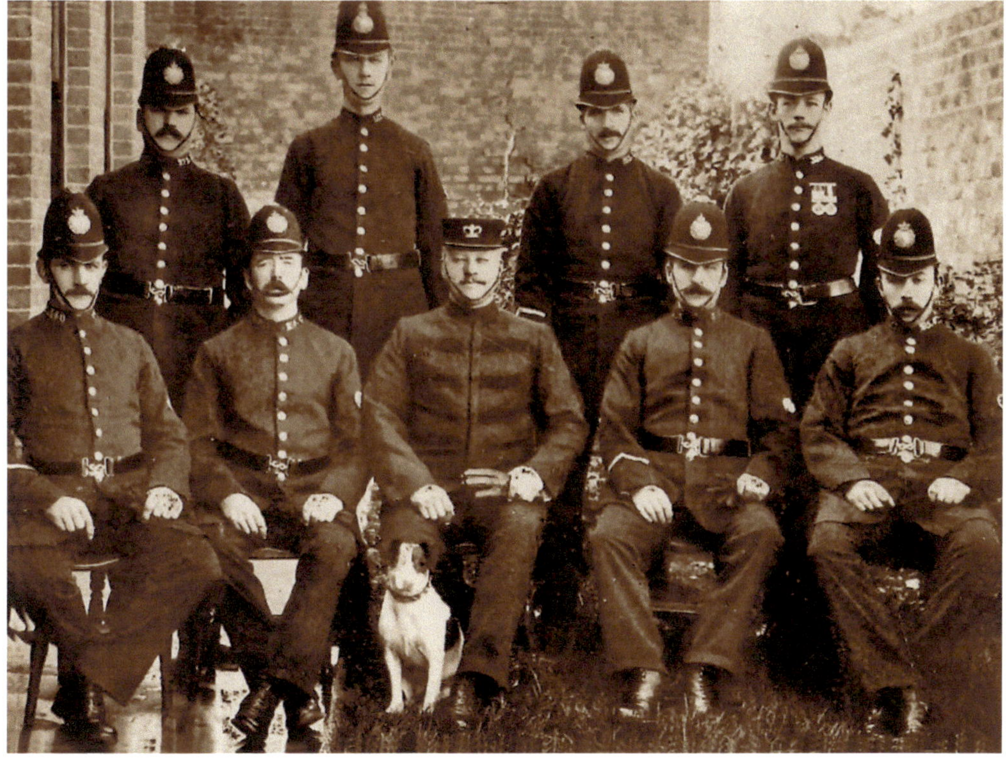

Tewkesbury Division Police Force, 1904. PC Kenny standing far left (back row).

action, or a lower form of larceny' than robbing church offertory boxes placed there for charitable purposes and the benefit of the poor. PC Thomas Kenny was given a special commendation for his arrest.

An earlier case of pecuniary impropriety also occurred in 1830 when William Hale, a nailer, who fulfilled the role of steward of the New Unity Society of Tewkesbury, which met at the Duke of York inn (now closed), No. 8 Barton Street, was convicted of stealing thirty-nine sovereigns from funds collected by this friendly society for the relief of sick members and their families. After being sentenced to transportation for life the judge commented that Hale displayed much dextrous ingenuity that could have been put to much better use.

DID YOU KNOW?
In 1893 Henry Harrison was convicted at Tewkesbury Police Court of stealing a bottle of claret from the Bell Hotel. The eighteen-year-old repeat offender was initially suspected by the landlady, who saw Harrison at the bar shortly before the bottle went missing from the counter. The crucial evidence came from a passer-by who saw Harrison hiding the bottle in a cart full of grains that he drove away. Furthermore, once the empty bottle was retrieved it still bore traces of its hiding place. Harrison was sentenced to three months' hard labour.

4. Trade and Industry

While Tewkesbury has many trades typically found in any small market town, its medieval heritage and unique riverine position have led to the development of some unusual cottage industries – from tanning to nail making, and the production of tobacco and mustard.

Tanneries

Today, it is interesting to reflect that the eastern bank of the Mill Avon, now dominated by car parks and high-quality housing, once accommodated a highly profitable tanning industry. The name of Tannery Court is one of the few clues indicating that most of the land on the Mill Avon side of St Mary's Lane and Church Street (behind the elegant houses of the frontage) was once dominated by tannery companies as well as one chemical factory. Originally dating from the medieval period, when, in 1386, for example, the abbey's tannery sold as many as 373 hides, the town's tanning industry almost disappeared entirely by the end of the nineteenth century. Thereafter, its buildings were developed to serve successor industries. The St Mary's Tannery, for example, famously owned by the local miser Edmund Rudge, was replaced by the Halifax Manufactory – so named after Mrs Craik's famous novel *John Halifax, Gentleman* – before being occupied by Tannery Court *c.* 2016. A tannery owned by Nathaniel Hartland, on the other hand, who may have inspired Mrs Craik's character, the Quaker tanner Abel Fletcher, was initially converted into Tewkesbury's first factory making mass-produced boots and shoes. By 1856, however, Hartland had bought a better plot, which stretched from Church

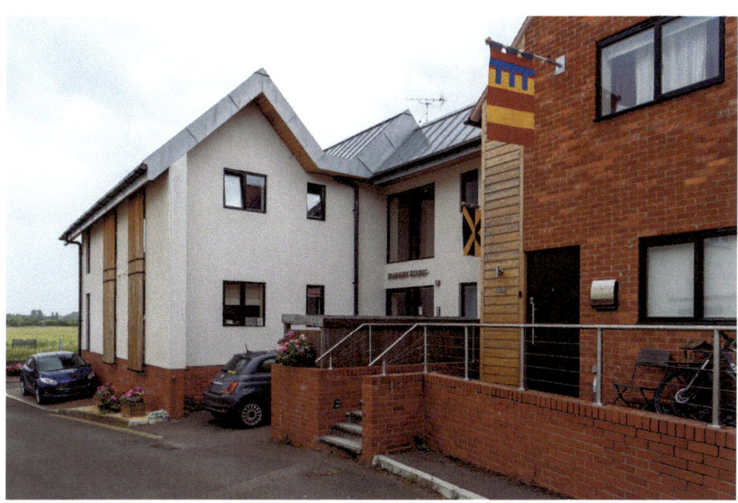

Tannery Court.

Street to the Mill Avon, leaving sufficient space behind an elegant town house to build a modern tannery. Today, the site is located at No. 97 Church Street, which, since 1917, has accommodated the YMCA.

DID YOU KNOW?
The political journalist William Cobbett visited Tewkesbury in 1830 to campaign against agricultural labourers' poor working conditions. Nevertheless, the audience, who were being charged a shilling per head for the privilege of hearing Cobbett talk about their suffering, was not impressed. As the local historian James Bennett recorded, Cobbett, after becoming irate about some who started to make a din, 'called upon the gallery people to come down and turn the disturbers out of the house; but the company in the boxes exhibiting a disposition to support their neighbours in the pit, the "gods" thought fit to disregard the orator's invitation'.

Hartland's tannery prospered greatly, to the extent that some of the wealth generated was used to build a Quaker church and school, subsequently redeveloped as the Watson Hall. The Hartlands also bought the Gloucestershire Banking Company in 1838 to form Hartland's Bank. However, in the long term this expansion proved unhelpful for Tewkesbury as Nathaniel Hartland decided to expand his horizons through buying Ashley Manor (now St Edward's Preparatory School, Cheltenham), a grand mansion in Charlton Kings, to where his wealth was subsequently directed. Thereafter, the tannery declined and was sold off to become a shirt factory in 1890. Although no visible signs of the town's tannery industry remain today, one theory suggests that the Grade II listed, *c.*1800 building, currently described by Historic England as a 'gazebo' (now the Riverside Café), constructed with Flemish bond brick adjacent to the River Avon, was an office building originally used by the tannery. Perhaps the real identity of this enigmatic building will be revealed in the future.

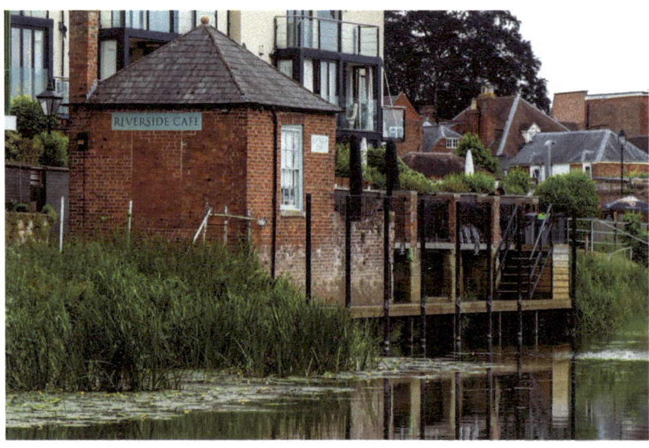

The mysterious gazebo, possibly once used by the tanning industry.

Mustard Making

A visible reminder of the town's long association with the production of mustard can be seen at Nos 13–14 Barton Street (currently occupied by Kellands Financial Advisors). Known as The Mustard House, the building dates back to the fifteenth century when mustard seed was dried in the gabled roof and the finished products sold from the ground floor. The mustard was rolled into balls for convenience of transportation and storage after being infused with horseradish for added pungency. By the sixteenth century Tewkesbury had become established as an important centre for mustard making, the ingredients being found in profusion along local river banks and in the surrounding meadows. Legend even suggests that mustard balls covered in gold leaf were presented to Henry VIII and Anne Boleyn when they visited Tewkesbury on 26 July 1535 during their Royal Progress tour. By 1662, the historian Thomas Fuller pronounced that Tewkesbury mustard was the 'best in England'. Such was their 'fiery' nature that Tewkesbury mustard balls were even once used as a metaphor for incendiary fireballs as part of the conspiracy theory that the Great Fire of London (1666) was started by Catholic arsonists, rather than by accident.

Indeed, Tewkesbury mustard achieved such fame and popularity through its strong, sharp characteristics that it started infiltrating everyday language and our national literature. Various proverbs arose, including 'He looks as if he had liv'd on Tewksbury mustard', which the antiquary Francis Grose explained as referring to 'any peevish or snappish person, or one having a cross, fierce, or ill-natured contenance', the assumption being that anyone eating it would soon assume these qualities. This predisposition

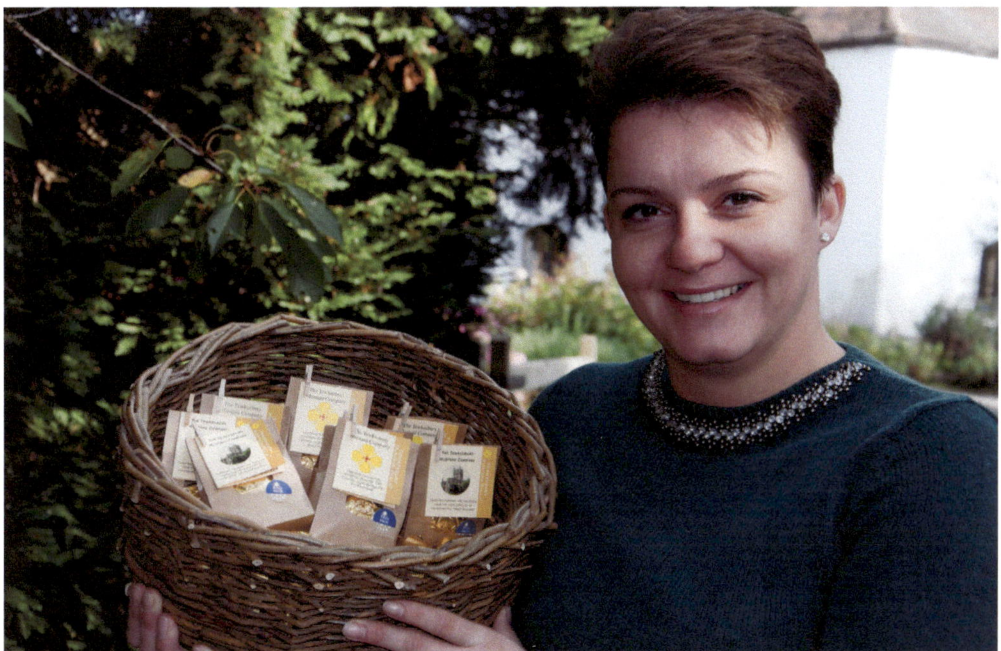

Mustard balls produced by the Tewkesbury Mustard Company.

was also alluded to in *A Strange Metamorphosis of Man* (1634), attributed to Richard Braithwaite, who stated that a 'true Tewxbury man ... is a cholerick gentleman, [who] will bear no coals', and, later, by James Bennett in *The History of Tewkesbury* (1830), who suggested it can be 'applied to those prigs who exhibit a more than ordinary degree of pertness'. William Shakespeare would have been acquainted with these proverbs and the jocular use of Tewkesbury mustard as a metaphor for biting characteristics. He used it to comic effect in Act 2, Scene 4 of *Henry IV Part II* (*c.* 1598) when John Falstaff converses with the prostitute Doll Tearsheet about his friend 'Ned' Poins: 'He a good wit? hang him, baboon! his wit's as thick as Tewksbury mustard'.

The perceived ill effects of eating too much Tewkesbury mustard were also captured in art through the caricaturist and writer George Murgatroyd Woodward (*c.* 1760–1809). Ironically nicknamed 'Mustard George' on account of his middle name, Murgatroyd, being corrupted to 'Moutard' and then 'Mustard', Woodward made his mark through humorous portraits of members of the middle and lower classes. Inspired by the proverb 'He looks as sharp as Tewksbury mustard', Woodward drew two sharp-featured gentlemen for his Tewkesbury portraits, later etched by Isaac Cruickshank.

Following the advent of mass-produced foodstuffs during the nineteenth century, Tewkesbury mustard's cottage industry began to diminish, despite the efforts of E. Moore, the High Street chemist's, who, in 1852–53, promoted the sale of the mustard in jars, including bottles of its newly invented Tewkesbury Severn Sauce, described as possessing 'all the stimulating properties of the far-famed Tewkesbury mustard'. Today, however, the industry's authentic legacy is still kept alive by the Tewkesbury Mustard Company at Hoo House, Gloucester Road.

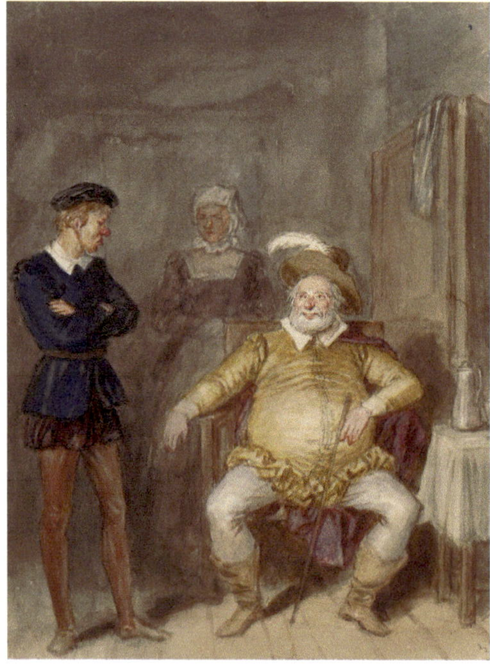

Illustration to Shakespeare's Falstaff plays, by John Massey Wright.

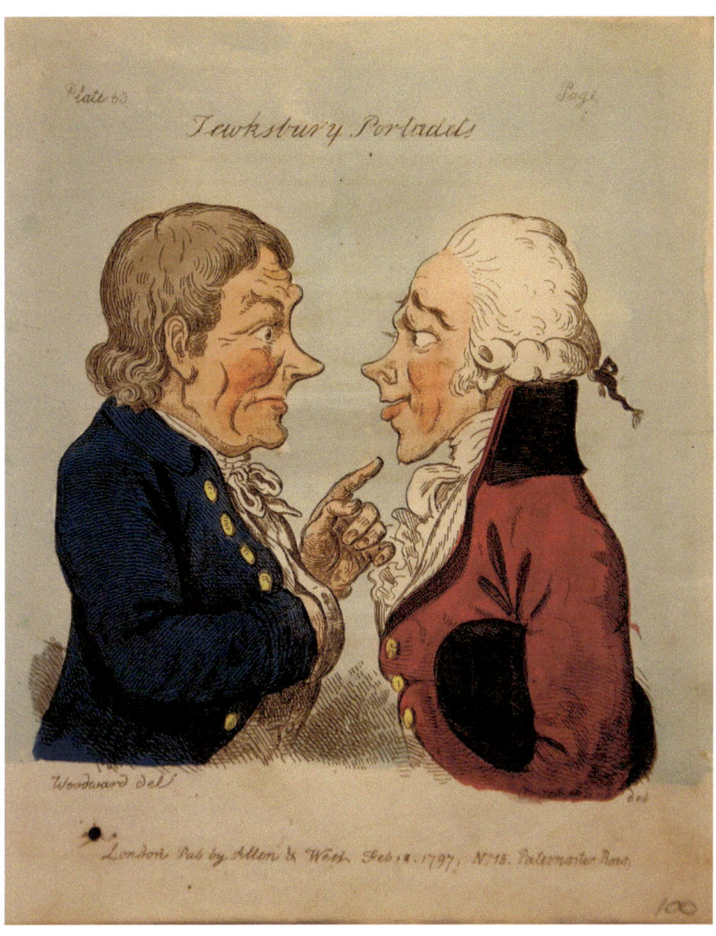

Tewksbury Portraits,
by Isaac Cruikshank
the Elder after George
Moutard Woodward,
1796–97.

Tobacco

Among the town's clandestine industries in the seventeenth century was the cultivation of tobacco. First brought to England in 1565, tobacco was introduced into the Gloucestershire area around 1619 and grown particularly in the triangle between Winchcombe, Cheltenham and Tewkesbury. Although King James I, under pressure to protect the interests of colonial planters in Virginia and Maryland, declared tobacco cultivation illegal in December 1619, the practice continued, its popularity partly arising through providing employment opportunities for poor labourers. While explicit orders were given in 1627 to destroy the town's tobacco crops, nine years later, Charles I's Privy Council discovered that it was still being grown on a large scale, with much produce being sold in the town or secretly transported to London. Just how palatable the early tobacco was is not known, but one consumer, a tapster employed in a Tewkesbury inn in the 1630s, reportedly referred to the licensee's tobacco as 'old vermine tobacco'. This was probably the product being sold by Thomas Crumpe, the town's first recorded tobacconist who became the sole tobacco licensee, though it was also available, for a time, from drinking premises run by a Thomas Sweeper.

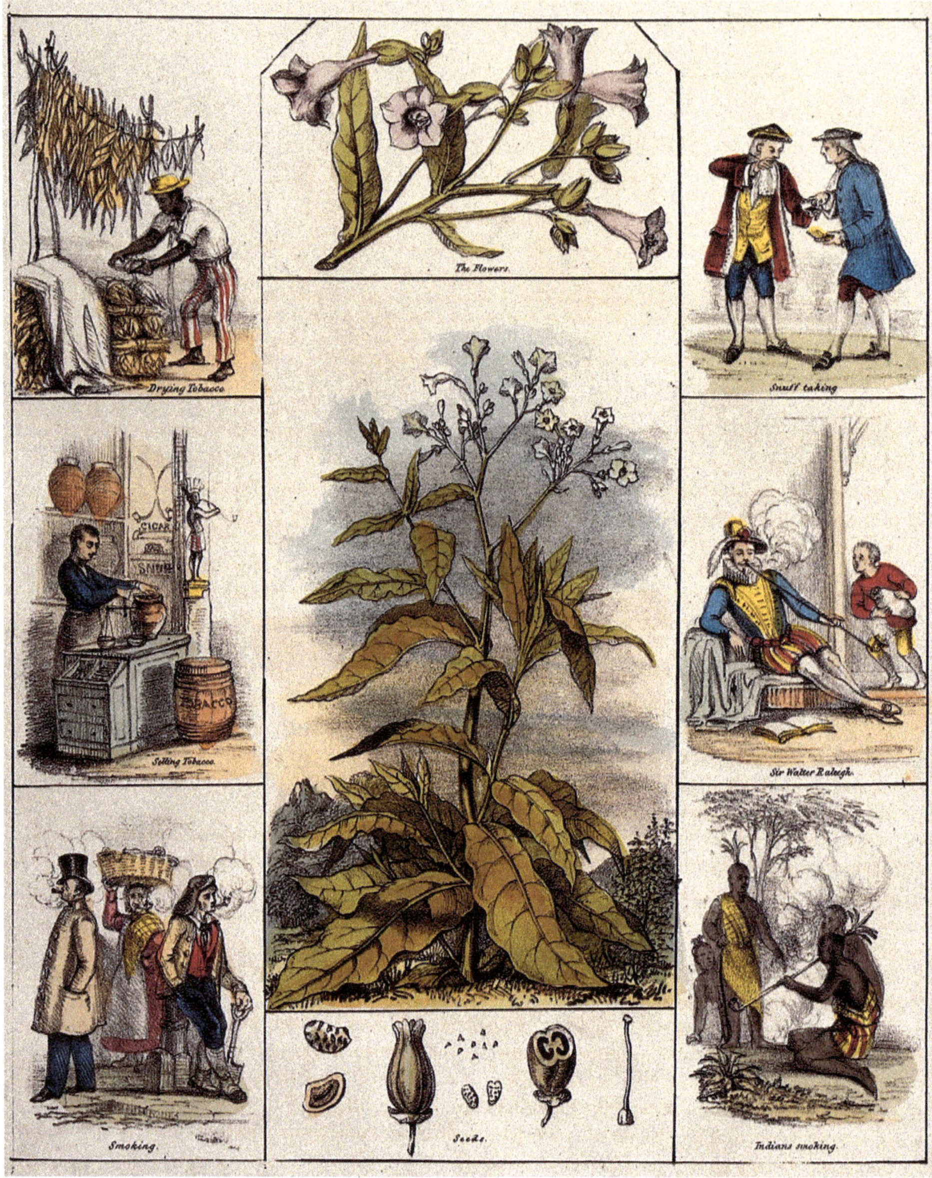

Tobacco plant (*Nicotiana tabacum*) and its uses, *c.* 1840.

Following the investigation, the Privy Council commanded the local bailiffs (an obsolete term for mayor of which Tewkesbury boasted two until 1835) to order the constables 'to pull up by the roots all the said tobacco' and enforce the ban properly through convicting any delinquents. Despite this and a 1652 Act, which expressly prohibited the planting of tobacco in England, the constable of Tewkesbury was prosecuted in 1664 for failing to destroy the crops. However, by the end of the 1680s, following mass production of cheaper Virginia tobacco, the local trade became less profitable and production soon diminished.

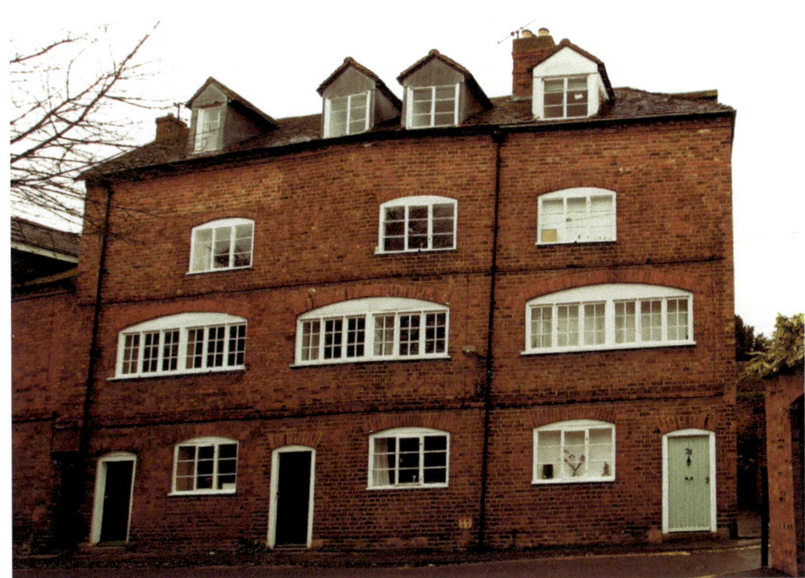

The recently restored weavers' cottages in St Mary's Lane.

Nail Making

Nail making had been established as one of the town's core industries from at least the eighteenth century, one of the principal areas of activity being centred at the bottom of Tolsey Lane, where shops by the Avon in Nailor's Square (also known as the Quadrangle, now demolished) were once located. The work was hard, highly skilled and usually undertaken in filthy environments. Practitioners were reputedly able to handcraft as many as 250 nails per hour from iron bars. In 1805 the Quadrangle's reputation was called into question when the Revd Edmund Butcher published an account of his journey from Sidmouth to Chester via Tewkesbury. Referring to the nailers, he commented they were 'so rude and savage that it was scarcely deemed safe for the other inhabitants to go into their quarter'. Later on, given some evidence of legal cases involving nailers, which led to their transportation to Australia, perhaps there was some justification for this remark.

Another prime location for the trade was on the north side of Barton Street, where it once led into Nailor's Alley (demolished when Nelson Street was built, *c.* 1855). So called because of the preponderance of nail-making shops located there, the alley was owned by the ironmonger Samuel Barnes. Given the fact that women and children were also employed in the trade, Barnes installed forges in the tenants' kitchens so that entire families could be productive in their homes. Shortly before his death in 1830 Barnes used some of his wealth to build a block of almshouses (demolished in the late 1950s) in Chance Street, on the site now occupied by Spring Gardens sheltered accommodation. One wonders if any of the nailers, whose handiwork may have been used as part of its construction, became deserving cases to live there. By 1835, following the impact of the Industrial Revolution on many cottage industries, only around fifty people were still employed in the trade. Attempts to establish pin factories, firstly, in 1849, near the bottom of High Street, and then, three years later, in Oldbury, were short-lived, the latter a possible forerunner of the Oldbury Engineering Works. In 1895, when the ninety-five-year-old James Hill died, *The Tewkesbury Register* reported the loss of the last remaining link with an industry which was once carried out on a large scale.

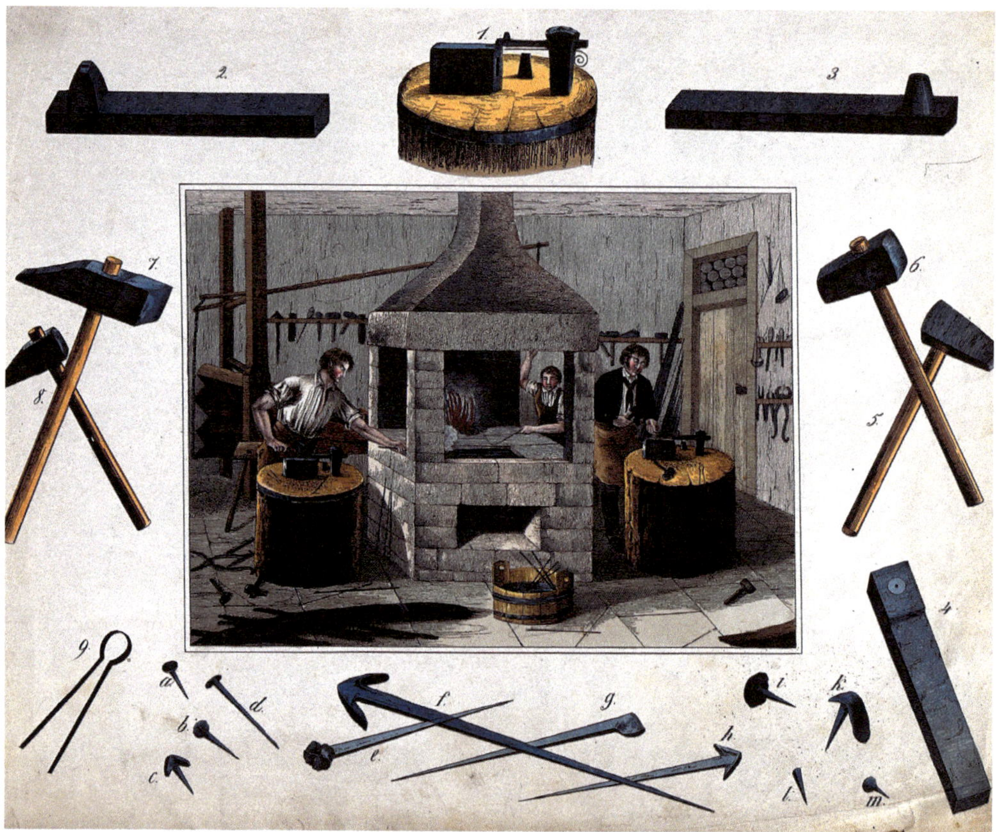

Some of the tools used for making nails and pins of various sizes.

The Undeveloped Spa

Among the town's more unusual enterprising ventures, but perhaps doomed to fail from the start, were attempts to exploit mineral water in the Lower Lias around Walton House, either side of the A38. Threatening to rival its Cheltenham Spa neighbour, plans to create an inland resort there first surfaced in 1746. As noted by the antiquarian Samuel Rudder, a well was sunk in 1750 'to enable the people of Tewkesbury to enjoy the benefits of [Walton's] purging water'. The original well was located in the grounds of Walton House (located off Churchill Grove), built by Nicholas Smithsend in 1790 shortly before his death. Another well was sunk in a field to the north of the A38 and Walton House. According to Bigland, writing in 1786–91, the pump room, with four-columned Doric portico, was built in this field *c.*1749.

Keen to revive the Walton water, Smithsend commissioned the eminent Worcester physician Dr James Johnstone to publish a treatise on the health benefits of the water in 1787. Almost anticipating the meteoric rise in Cheltenham's fortunes that would arise from King George III's visit there the following year, Johnstone went to great lengths to forestall potential future objections, commenting in the preface that while the properties and medicinal powers of Walton water were almost identical to Cheltenham's, it would not harm its reputation. On the contrary, he wrote:

> . . . it will be a Satisfaction to Invalids to be assured of having within a small Distance, a Water of the same Kind, to which recourse may be had, when the Numbers are so great at Cheltenham, as to be insufficiently supplied from the Well there.

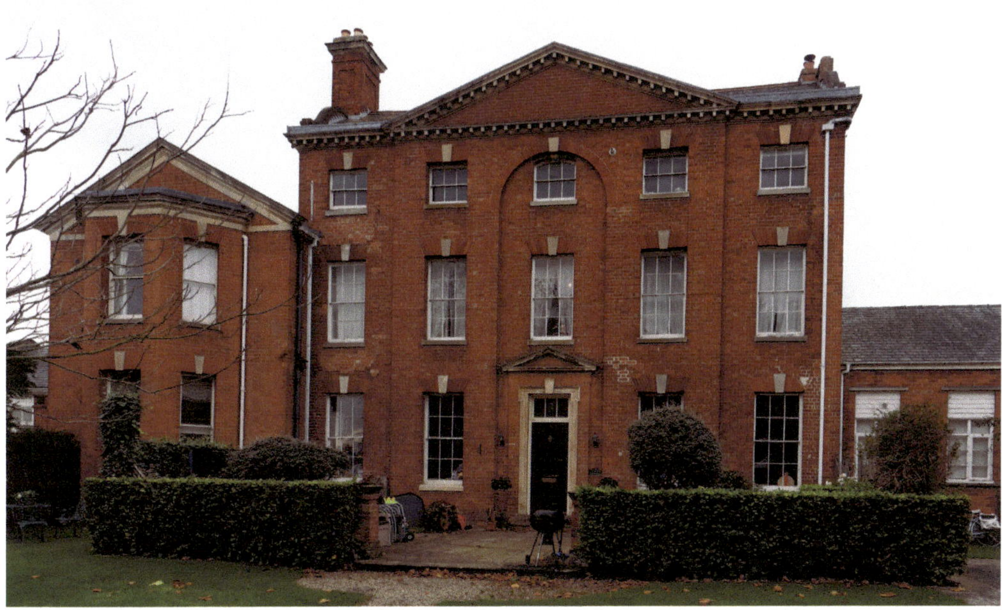

Walton House.

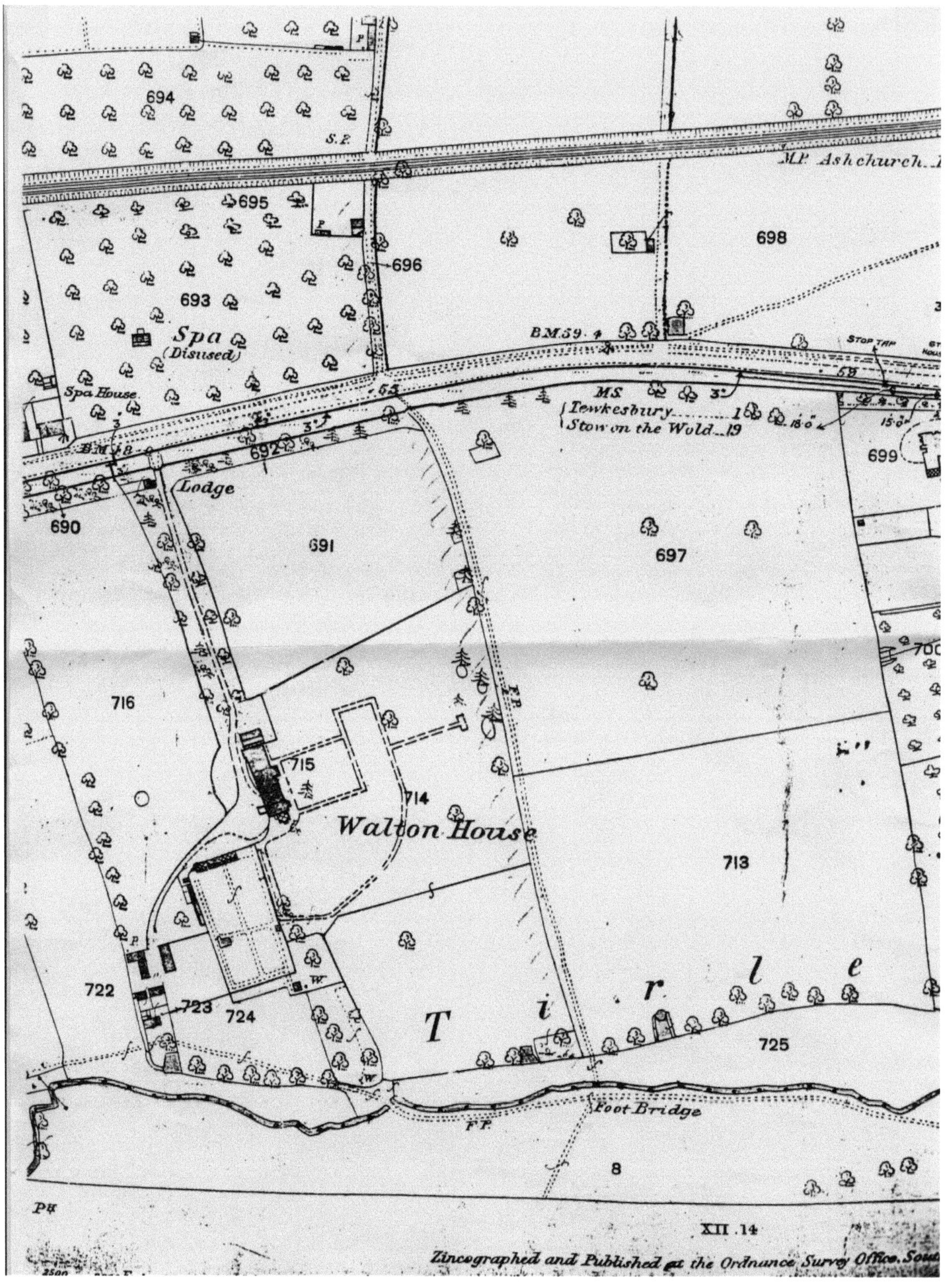

The original location of the spa and the spa house.

SOME ACCOUNT

OF THE

WALTON WATER,

NEAR

TEWKESBURY;

WITH

Thoughts on the Use and Diseases

OF THE

LYMPHATIC GLANDS.

IN A LETTER

To J. COAKLEY LETTSOM, M.D. of the College of Physicians, Fellow of the Royal, Antiquary, and Medical Societies, LONDON.

BY JAMES JOHNSTONE, M.D.

PHYSICIAN to the GENERAL INFIRMARY, WORCESTER; FELLOW of the ROYAL MEDICAL SOCIETY, EDINBURGH; of the PHILOSOPHICAL SOCIETIES of MANCHESTER and BATH; and corresponding MEMBER of the MEDICAL SOCIETY, LONDON.

——Sacros Ausus recludere fontes.

WORCESTER:

PRINTED by J. TYMBS, at the CROSS; And sold by T. CADELL, Strand; C. DILLY, in the Poultry; T. BECKET, Pall-Mall, London; HARWARD, Tewkesbury, Gloucester, and Cheltenham; Messrs. EDDOWS, Shrewsbury; PEARSON and ROLLASON, Birmingham; RUDHALL, Bristol; PRATT, Bath; and JACKSON, Oxford.

1787

The treatise published by Dr James Johnstone.

Yet, while Cheltenham's spa prospered, another historian Thomas Fosbrooke, writing in 1807, warned that 'no Naiad will be worshipped [at Walton], till temples have been likewise erected to pleasure, convenience, and dissipation'. Nevertheless, such a development never occurred despite the efforts by local residents and boarding house owners who promoted the therapeutic qualities of the water. Although a spa house was built near the well c.1835, it failed to successfully exploit the mineral water. Then, following purchase of the rights to the use of the water by a group of Cheltenham businessmen, further serious efforts to revive the vision of a spa were only made once the Cheltenham rights to the water expired. In 1931, for example, it was suggested that Tewkesbury could model its development on the recent successes achieved by the smaller spas in North Wales, while in 1954, the idea resurfaced at the annual dinner of the Tewkesbury Chamber of Commerce especially as, it was reported, 'Cheltenham was losing, or had lost, its interest in the spa side'.

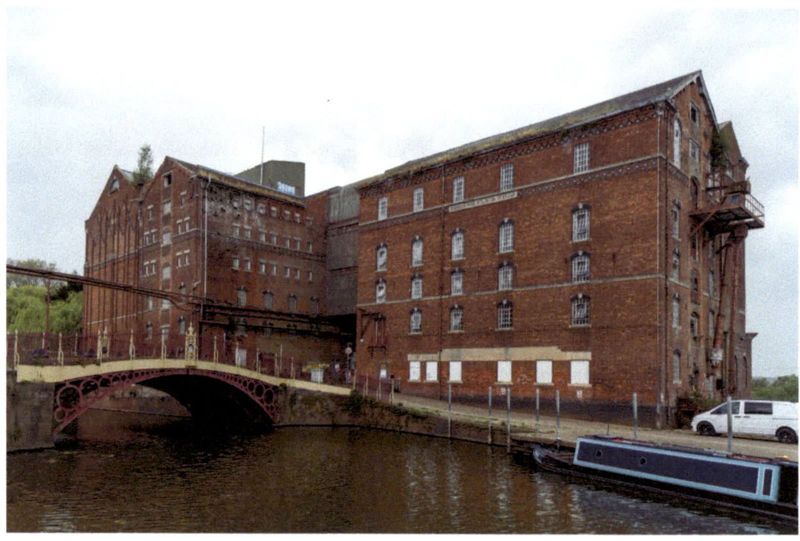

Healings
Mill today.

Even so, it was not to be. The pump room was demolished in 1961. Earlier, as discovered by research from Jill Waller, the Spa House became the Rose & Crown beerhouse, Northway/Ashchurch, from the 1830s until 1874. Since then, the site has been redeveloped as the Springfield and Wellfield estates. Although Walton spa water never became as celebrated as Cheltenham's, its therapeutic qualities, like those of its rival, were perhaps equally dubious. As Johnstone commented back in 1787: 'a Pint or more, acts as a gentle Laxative and Diuretic: And it occasions a slight giddiness in some persons, in others a sort of a heavy pain in the head'.

DID YOU KNOW?
Tewkesbury's flour mills were blocked by dead bats and a swarm of flies and bees on 24 July 1571 and on 24 February 1575 respectively. By 1892, Healings Mill was reputedly the largest and most advanced flour mill in the country, producing twenty-five sacks of flour an hour. Benefitting from access via three modes of transport – road, rail and canal/river – it carried on a tradition begun by the abbey's monks in the twelfth century who operated a watermill on the Avon. When the mill ceased on 20 October 2006, it ended 140 years of milling on that site.

Fairground Equipment

One of the town's more unusual trades, which lasted more than half a century, was the manufacture of fairground equipment. The agricultural iron-working firm of Thomas Walker & Sons was established in Oldbury Road in a former silk mill in 1871, initially employing just six people, but soon diversified into producing fairground equipment

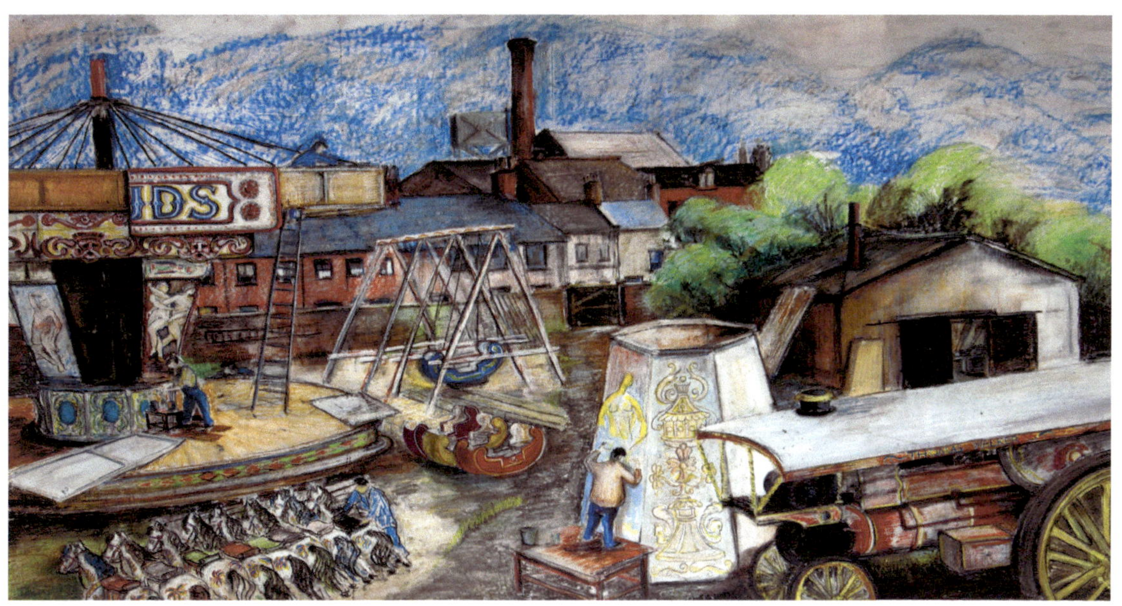

The Works of T. Walker & Sons, by Percival Stephen Braisby.

for home and foreign markets, including for the famous Tivoli Gardens in Copenhagen. The trade started to develop through the firm's close proximity to the site of the town's annual Mop Fair after travelling showmen approached Walker's to undertake occasional repair work.

The work involved considerable attention to detail, ingenuity, experimentation and innovation. The firm took out several British patents, including for the design of galloping horses on roundabouts, as the public's appetite for novel and inspiring attractions continued unabated. By 1908 the business employed around sixty workers, but was nearly totally destroyed when a fire on 2 September 1908 gutted the premises. Starting in the pattern room in the early hours of the morning, the fire raged for two hours, almost killing the Walker family while they slept in their residential quarters. Despite the considerable losses, including 5,000 irreplaceable casting patterns, the firm recovered, building a new factory on a 2-acre site adjacent to Holy Trinity Church, and thereby providing more space for constructing and testing the finished machines. Following Thomas's death in 1912 the firm was run by his wife Mary and their two sons, John and Alfred. By 1924 Walker's was one of only three firms employed in this specialist trade but was facing stiff competition from German and American counterparts. Estimating that his workforce could easily be doubled within six months were it not for foreign free trade, in an interview for *The Gloucestershire Chronicle* Alfred Walker complained about the excessively high export tariffs to the US, amounting to 75 per cent of the equipment's total cost. Perhaps unsurprisingly, the firm closed down shortly afterwards, depriving the town of the use of specialist skills.

5. Transport

It is interesting to reflect that the description of the town's transport infrastructure –
'above the Confluence of Avon and Severne' and with '3. Streates … meating at the Market
Crosse, wherof the chifiest is caullid the High Strete' – made by John Leland in the
sixteenth century is still recognisable to us today. While these features have remained the
same, other aspects of the town's transportation history have changed or become hidden.
These include the loss of its ancient ferry at Upper Lode, and the distant memories of its
railway stations and, prior to that, the coaches that once raced through the town.

Lost Ancient Ferry

Although the ferry at Lower Lode, just below the entry of the Mill Avon into the Severn,
is still easily located, the site of the ancient ferry at Upper Lode, also known as Overlode,
where the Severn was diverted to provide locks and a weir, is more difficult to identify.
Yet, well before Thomas Telford constructed the Mythe Bridge in 1826, the ferry provided
an important crossing point for farmers bringing their produce to Tewkesbury from the
Bushley/Longdon side of the Severn.

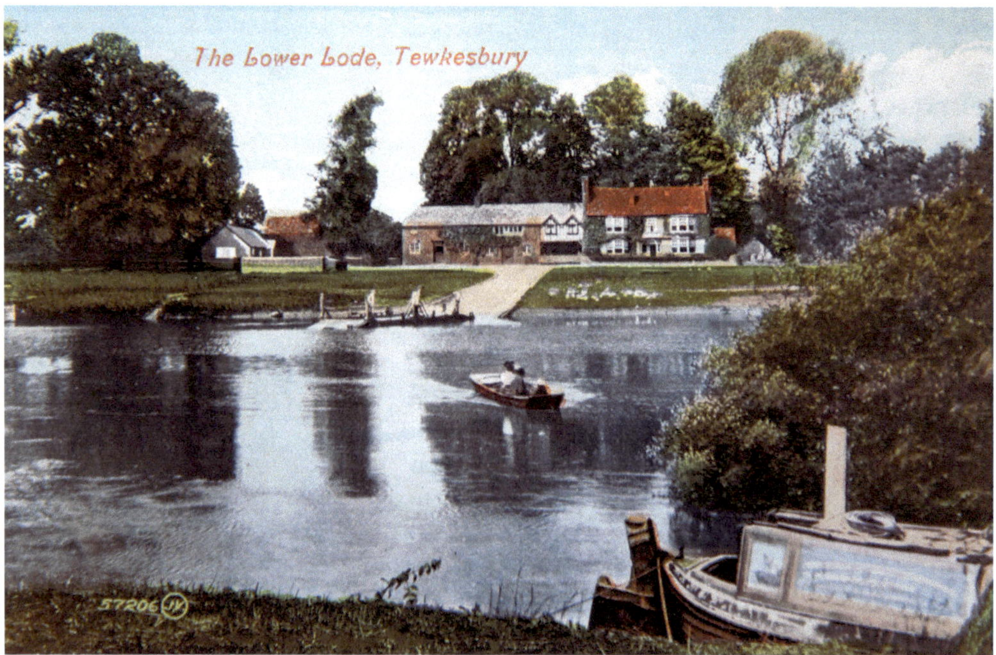

The ferry at Lower Lode.

Prior to the dissolution farmers had benefitted from paying an annual toll, through tithes, in sheaves of wheat, either a thrave (twenty-four sheaves) or a thrass (twelve sheaves), payable even in times of plague when the ferry was not operating. However, following the transfer of the ferry's rights to Nicholas Wyatt in 1542, the new owner sought to impose new tariffs. This led the locals in Bushley and Longdon to protest, taking the matter to court on 17 September 1624, where they gave evidence of the long-standing custom of a 'Passage Cart' visiting local farms after harvest to collect the tithes. Among the depositions made was one by John Tawney, who, after confirming the longevity of the ancient custom, recounted an incident about fifty years earlier when, after attempting to use the crossing, he was denied access by Walter Trigge, the then owner. In response, Dowdeswell drew his sword and used the boat, claiming that 'the passage was the Kings highway and that he was a customer'. Today, the site of the ferry can be located near the old ferry house, which traded variously as the Upper Lode Inn, the Ferry Inn, and the Dowdeswell Arms until its closure *c*.1858. Interestingly, the old river course is still visible here.

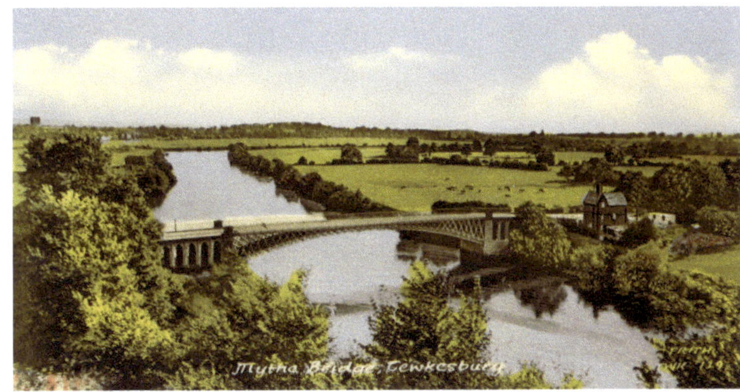

The Mythe Bridge, which possibly replaced the Overlode ferry in 1826.

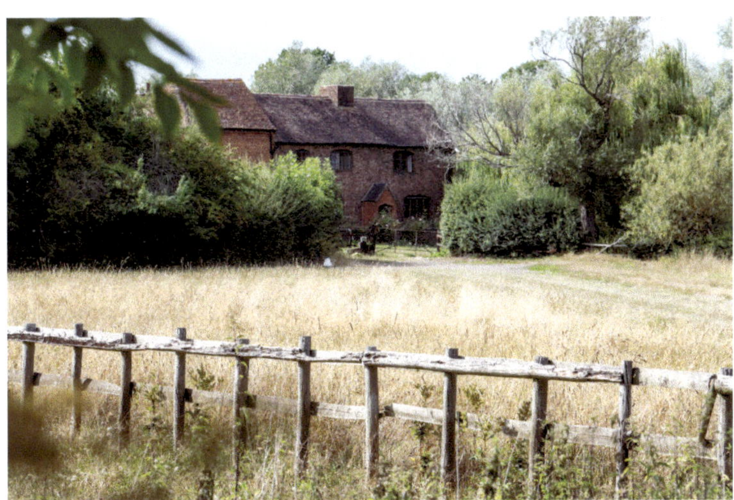

The old ferry house at Upper Lode.

'Golden Age' of Coach Travel

When Mr Pickwick dined at the Hop Pole in 1828 Tewkesbury's population was approaching around 5,780, an increase of about 16 per cent from 1821.The town was benefitting greatly from its location along the major road route from north to west. By 1830 the number of daily coach services operating through the town exceeded thirty. Apart from being able to change horses at the Swan and the Hop Pole, coaches also benefitted from numerous inns which sprung up to provide food and lodging. While the advent of the railways sounded the death knell to this 'golden age', for a while, coaches still tried to compete with them on speed.

As improvements to road surfaces were made possible in Gloucestershire from 1726 through the creation of turnpike trusts, the speed with which coaches could travel also began to accelerate. By the mid-nineteenth century, among the fastest horse-drawn coaches were the *L'Hirondelle* and *Hibernia.* Given that they operated along similar routes between Liverpool and Bristol a fierce rivalry broke out between them. Rarely losing sight of one another, they raced against each other all the way, coming together at Tewkesbury after following slightly divergent routes from Shrewsbury. James Bennett recorded that on 1 May 1833 *L'Hirondelle* covered the 122-miles distance from Birkenhead Ferry, Liverpool, to the Swan Hotel in Tewkesbury in less than nine hours. However, among the fastest stretches was the journey between Cheltenham and Tewkesbury, which the *L'Hirondelle* and *Hibernia* covered in thirty minutes, travelling on average at 16 miles per hour.

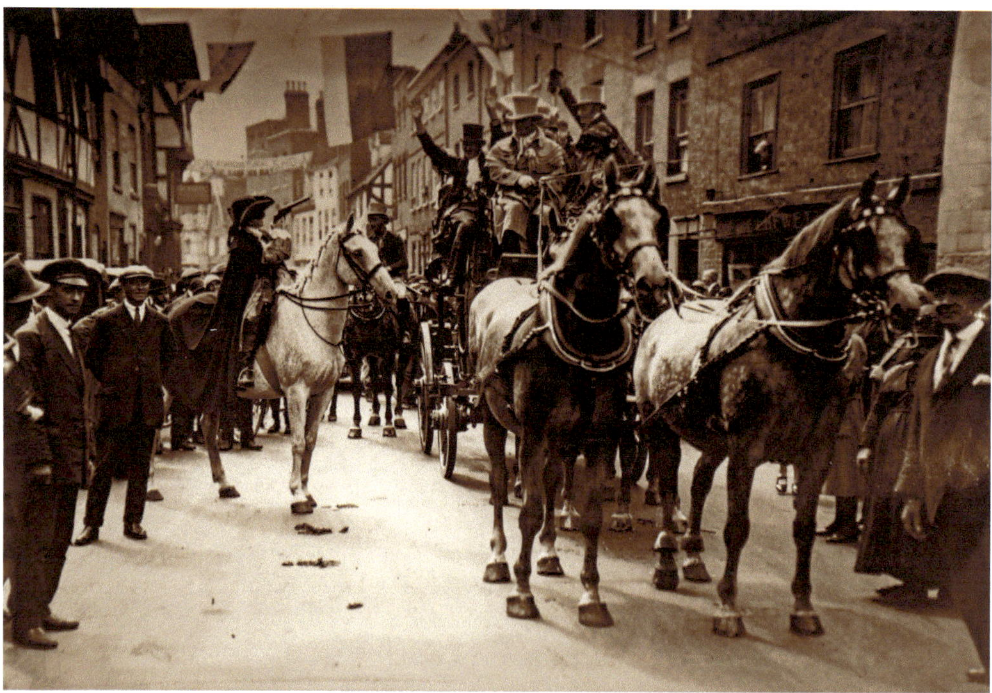

Centenary celebrations of *Pickwick Papers* in Tewkesbury, 28 July 1928.

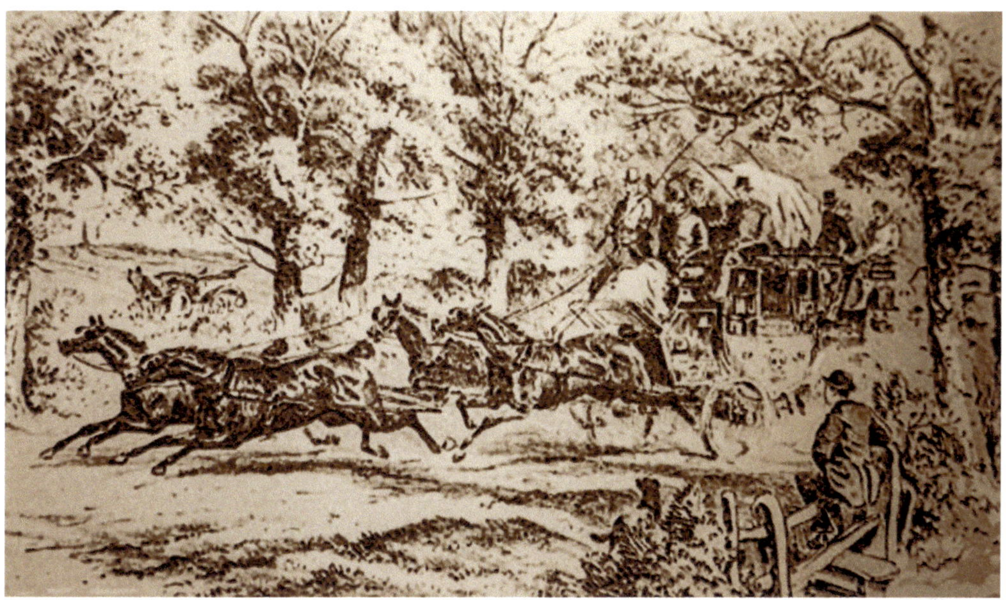

Galloped the 5-mile stage, in eighteen minutes, by John Sturgess.

DID YOU KNOW?
On 25 December 1739 a severe frost caused the Severn to become heavily frozen for nearly two months, during which laden wagons and horses were able to cross at the Upper and Lower Lode, while the services of the ferrymen were not required.

Nevertheless, although the horses were changed regularly at each planned stage along the way, Bennett expressed considerable sympathy for the horses, which, he felt, were being exploited 'merely to gratify the vanity of an unfeeling coachman'. His concerns were fully justified: on 30 April 1835 he reported how the *L'Hirondelle* horses suffered a terrible accident when descending the hill near the house of industry (now Shephard Mead) at half-past six in the morning. After the coach hit the post of a turnpike gate, the driver was hurled from the box. While he and the passengers fortunately survived, one of the horses was so badly injured that it had to be put down straight away, with the other two suffering severe bruising. Another serious incident involved the *Paul Pry* four-horse stagecoach, which, according to the 1924 recollections of centenarian, Mrs Sarah Fletcher, sometimes conveyed 'prisoners for Transportation'. The accident occurred on 17 May 1838 on the journey from London to Worcester. Perhaps the horses had become so conditioned to speeding off, that they bolted away from their stop at the Anchor Inn immediately after the carriage had been attached, but before the coachman and passengers had properly settled into their seats. After being prevented from continuing along its usual route at the top of the High Street the *Paul Pry* sped off towards Bredon but was eventually stopped at Kemerton Hill, about 4 miles to the north-east. According to Bennett the only passenger was 'an elderly female, who steadily retained her seat on the roof, and escaped without injury.'

Those who travelled on these coaches were drawn largely from the middle class, given that the upper classes usually owned their own coaches, while cost prevented the lower classes from using this form of transport. Unsurprisingly, ticket prices varied considerably depending on whether one travelled inside the carriage or on the outside. In 1838 'very reduced fares' were advertised for the *L'Hirondelle* coach of £1 15*s* (inside) and 17*s* (out) to travel from Liverpool to Cheltenham. Choosing the latter, however, was not without risk. On Christmas Eve 1836, for example, three passengers on the outside of a coach travelling from Tewkesbury to Bath were found frozen to death. Other risks included highway robbers or even murderers as fellow passengers. Among the gruesome incidents was one which occurred on 11 January 1840 when a quarryman called Richard Yarworth was shot twice by one of the passengers who had travelled with him from Worcester to Tewkesbury. After stopping at the Black Bear Inn the coach proceeded to Coombe Hill where it dropped off Yarworth so that he could walk to Cheltenham. The suspect also decided to walk with Yarworth but, after walking for about 400 yards, pulled a pistol and shot him, robbing him of his money and watch. Although Yarworth survived the attack, he died seven months later. His assailant was later transported for fifteen years after being found guilty of another crime committed on the same day.

Although Tewkesbury's heritage of coach travel has now faded from memory, in 1960, Jim Gardner, the proprietor of the Wheatsheaf (at No. 132 High Street), bought a nineteenth-century Park Drag, which he named *The Tewkesbury Flier*. Although Gardner intended to establish a larger collection of coaches in the town, his plans were dashed after seven youths overturned *The Tewkesbury Flier* and damaged it beyond repair. The days of coach travel were truly numbered.

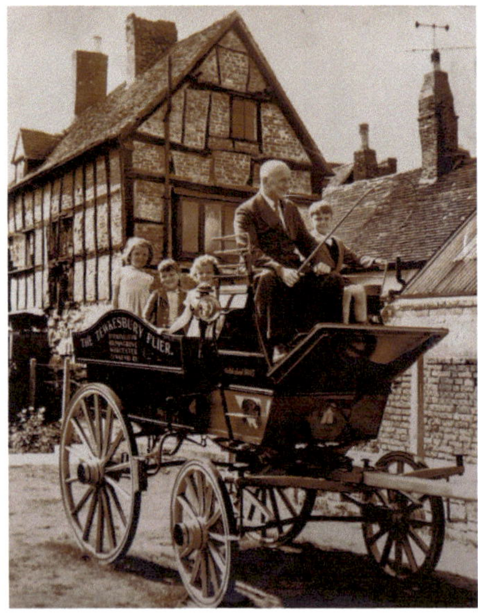

The Tewkesbury Flier, 1960.

The Lost Railway

Although many saw Tewkesbury's future economic development inextricably linked with the advent of the railway, others vehemently opposed the modernisation that this might bring. One commentator at Tewkesbury, for example, decried the potentially injurious nature of the railways, comparing railway engines to 'war-horses and fiery meteors' and contending that 'the evils contained in Pandora's box were but trifles compared with those that would be consequent on railways'. However, when the railway finally arrived in Tewkesbury in 1840 as the terminus of a Birmingham & Gloucester Railway branch line from Ashchurch, followed by a further rail extension to the quay soon afterwards, the contents of 'Pandora's box' appeared rather innocuous: given that there were four level-crossings in Tewkesbury, three of which were located in the town centre, steam locomotives were prohibited on the line until 1844 because of the risk they posed to pedestrians. Instead, as the *Tewkesbury Examiner* explained, passengers were conveyed 'in a handsome and convenient carriage drawn by one horse at good speed'. Despite this, an exception to this rule was made on 18–19 July 1843 when a small locomotive was provided to transport around 2,000 passengers to and from the town to attend the horse races being held on the Ham. Nevertheless, disaster almost struck when the train, then being driven by the company's locomotive superintendent, lost control after not stopping at Tewkesbury station, and nearly ended up in the River Avon after crossing the High Street and careering down the Quay branch line.

DID YOU KNOW?
On 5 September 1829 a hen boarded and concealed herself in a horse carriage, which had stopped in Tewkesbury. When the coach arrived in Cheltenham it was discovered that the hen had made a nest in the folds of the gentleman's travelling cloak and laid an egg there.

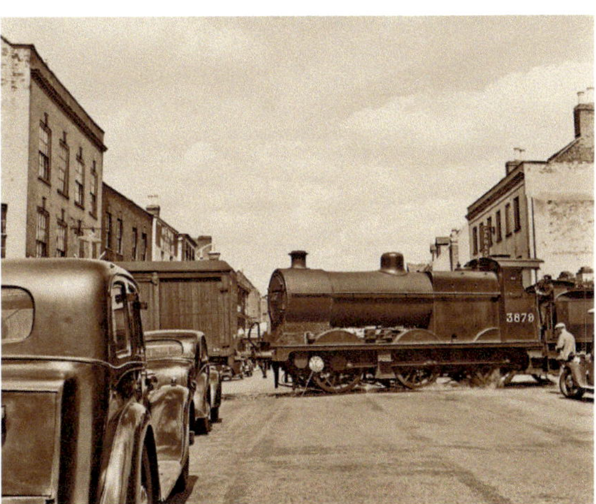

Engine 3879 crossing the High Street in late 1940s.

Today, it comes as a surprise to visitors to discover the plaque installed by Tewkesbury Railway and Historic Societies next to a single limestone column at No. 103 High Street, which marks all that remains of the town's first railway station. Originally completed by August 1839, the Gothic-style, 38-feet-wide building, built of Postlip freestone by the local contractor Thomas Phillips Holder, included a 133-feet-long platform at the rear. Yet, by 1864 the station had closed. The final ignominy occurred on 17 November 1846. As a train was pulling into the High Street station, the engine driver failed to engage the brake properly, causing one of the carriages to become disengaged from the engine. After careering through the closed station doors the carriage continued at speed, crossing the High Street and proceeding down Quay Lane (now Quay Street), before toppling over into the mud as frightened passengers jumped for their lives.

In the same year the old railway station was replaced by a new one serving the Tewkesbury & Malvern Railway. This was located to the north-east, some way from the town centre. Among the more unusual passengers carried from this station was a dog travelling solo. Details of this came to light through a case heard at Tewkesbury County Court when Arthur H. Collins, of Avon Lock House, brought a claim against the London, Midland & Scottish Railway Company for £2. The incident occurred on 31 December 1937 when Collins had taken his dog, a greyhound lurcher, to Tewkesbury railway station and paid 1s 4d, which included a premium, to send his dog to Haresfield at the company's risk. The journey involved two changes, at Ashchurch and Cheltenham. Unfortunately, however, the dog went missing at Cheltenham station where it had to wait around half an hour for its connection. Although witnesses testified that it was still chained to a platform bench just before the train arrived, it was thought that it became frightened by the approaching train and slipped its collar, leaving its collar and chain still attached to the bench. Making the case for the defence the solicitor pointed out 'that the company were not common carriers of dogs, and the loss was not due to the negligence of the company or its servants'. Although the judge expressed sympathy for Collins, he agreed that the company was not negligent and, therefore, found in their favour, concluding that the collar was probably insufficiently tightened.

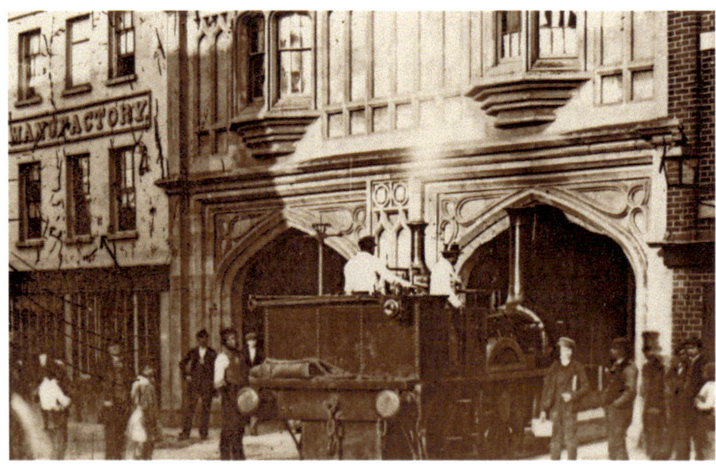

The earliest known photograph of Tewkesbury's High Street railway station.

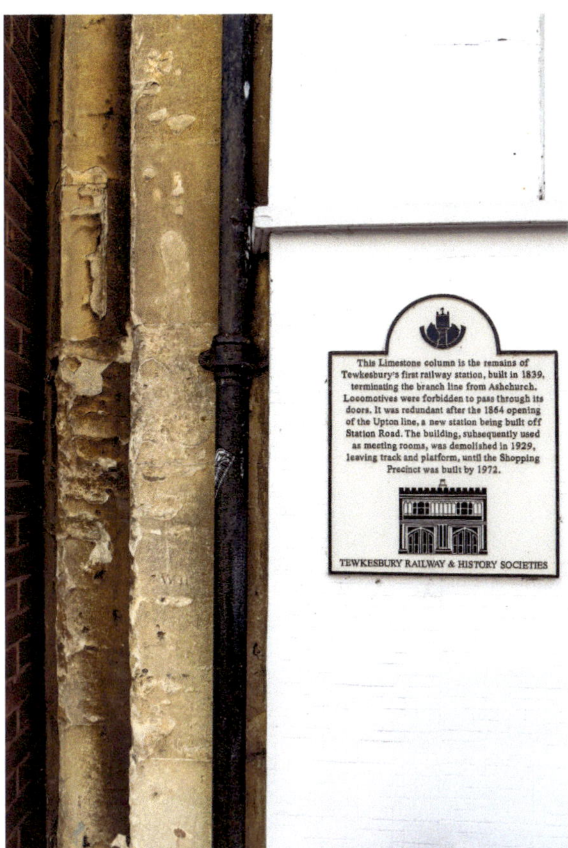

The plaque next to part of the limestone column.

Tewkesbury's second station closed in 1961. Today, the only clue of its existence is a raised bank covered in vegetation, where the platform once stood, located along the cycle path which adjoins Station Road behind Morrisons supermarket car park. For the Tewkesbury commentator, who feared 'war-horses and fiery meteors', the story of the town's railways was one of slow and gentle development and decline, while for its supporters the railways failed to kickstart significant economic growth. Indeed, one journalist in 1841 considered that its introduction had 'hitherto been one of almost unmixed evil to the inhabitants of Tewkesbury'.

DID YOU KNOW?
A number of elm trees in the area were used as prominent landmarks to describe roads to be turnpiked. Although the original trees have now disappeared their names survive: examples include Isabel's elm in Ashchurch, now marked by a house called 'The Elms', and Piff's Elm, the name still used for the road junction at the Gloucester Old Spot pub in Elmstone Hardwicke.

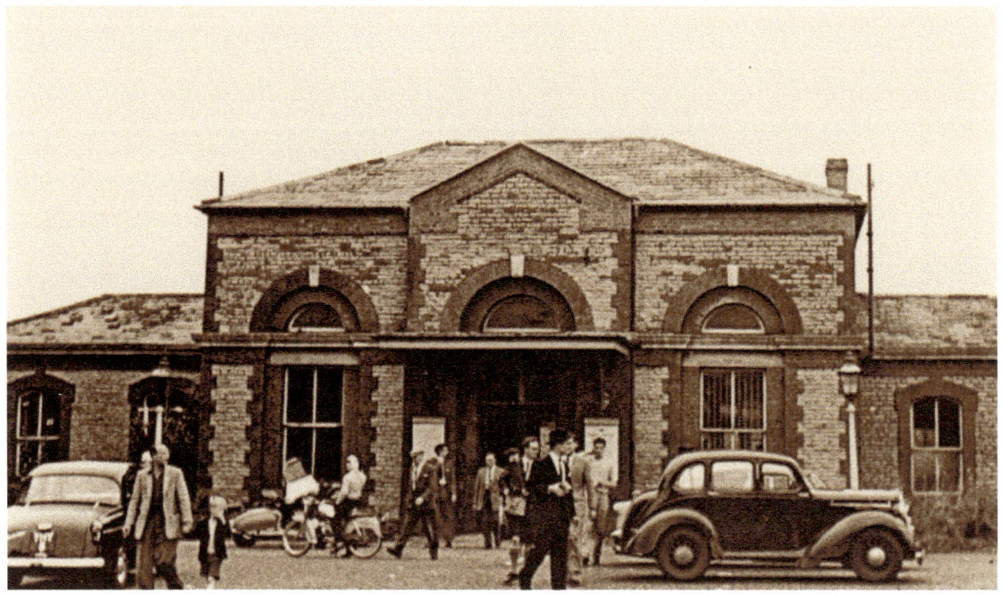

Nostalgic crowds leave the station for the last time, 12 August 1961.

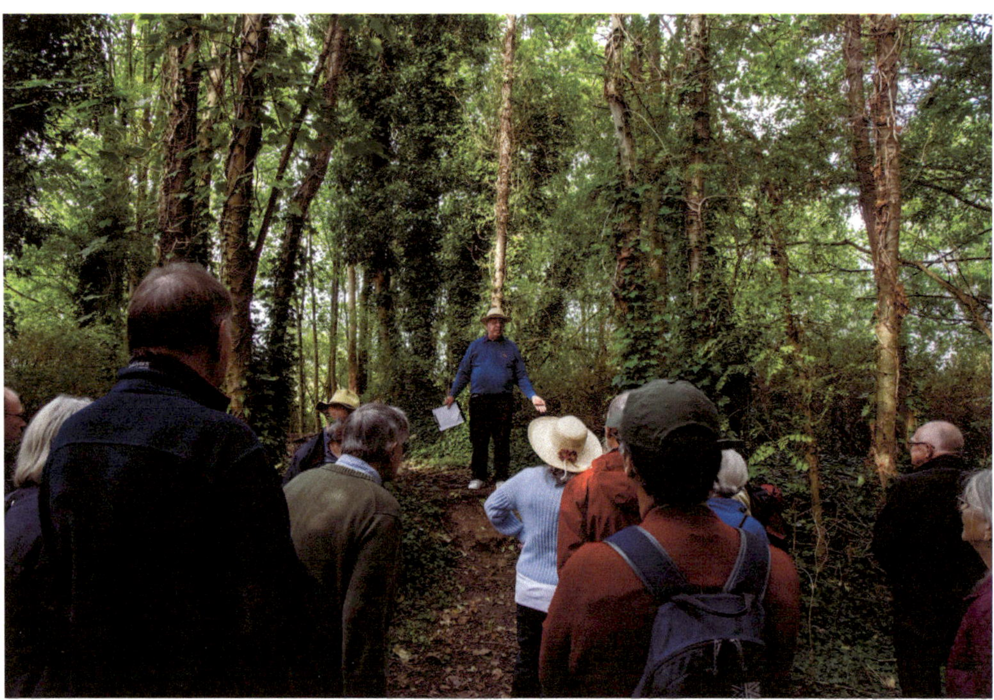

Site of the second railway station along the cycle path that adjoins Station Road.

6. Leisure and Entertainment

Over the years, the townsfolk have enjoyed a wide range of leisure pursuits, often utilising the resources on their doorstep, from rowing and swimming in the local rivers to attending races across the Ham's extensive acres. At times, the entertainment value has increased through the appearance of memorable characters, including the first man on record to row across the English Channel or the German pilot who once chased young boys and grazing cattle across the Ham in his Bleriot monoplane.

Horse Racing

One of the town's most popular pastimes, particularly between 1721 and 1846, was horse racing, a sporting and social event which thrilled Johanna Schopenhauer, *née* Trosiener (1766–1838), the German writer and mother of the German philosopher Arthur Schopenhauer, when she visited Tewkesbury as part of her travels in England and Scotland at the beginning of the nineteenth century. Such was its popularity in 1803 that she commented that the event attracted 'the whole of Cheltenham', a town later steeped in its own racing traditions. Among the other entertainments she witnessed were balls, a temporary theatre and rope dancers accompanied with enticing Turkish music.

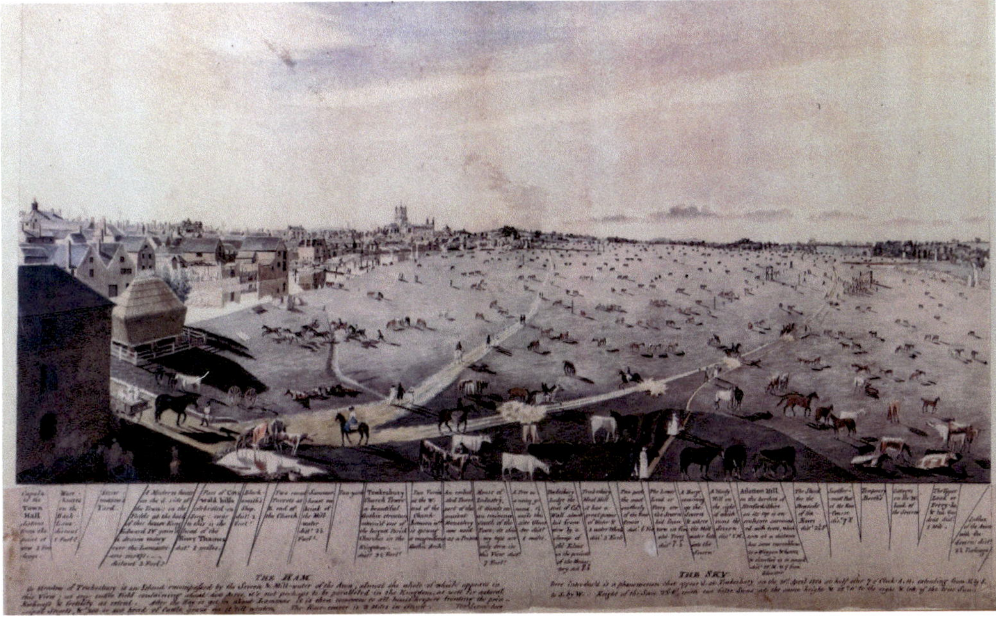

Racing on the Severn Ham.

Among the famous steeplechase riders to have won a race at Tewkesbury was Adam Lindsay Gordon (1833–70), who later became the national poet of Australia. Nevertheless, some local opposition to the races and the fact that they took place on the ancient meadow land of the Ham, prone to frequent flooding, led to their ultimate demise. Among the races' most vehement of critics was the evangelical rector Francis Close (1797–1882), whose dominance in Cheltenham led Tennyson to dub him the town's 'Pope'. Published shortly before becoming life trustee of the town's Holy Trinity Church, Close's polemical pamphlet, *Tewkesbury Races, And Their Fruits* (1844) described scenes of 'Riot and Debauchery; Drunkenness, Fornication and Lewedness; Quarrelling and Fighting; Cursing, Swearing and Filthy Talking', exacerbated by hundreds of prostitutes and criminals 'let loose upon the population to pollute and plunder them!' Despite attempts being made to revive the races in 1870 and, again, in the late 1880s signed with a petition of 150 citizens and shopkeepers, they were rejected by the Trustees of the Tewkesbury Commons.

DID YOU KNOW?

In 1941 an elephant from a travelling circus, located in Swilgate Meadow, escaped from its cage at night and ran amok throughout the town centre. After frightening local policemen and residents at the Plough, then along High Street and Smith's Lane, where it destroyed a vine tree and ate food left for the pigs, the 'mountain of living flesh', as described by the *Tewkesbury Yearly Magazine*, then proceeded towards the brewery. However, it failed to partake of any beverages since, by then, the police had alerted the keepers, who secured the elephant in its cage and, later, marched it off to Worcester.

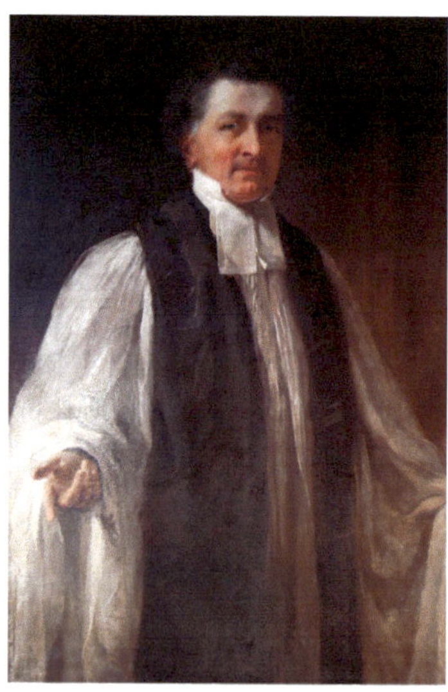

The evangelical rector Francis Close.

Rowing, Races and Regattas

Rowing as a competitive sport was established in Tewkesbury from at least 1835 when the Tewkesbury Sabrina Boat Club was formed and sponsored races held, including a 1-mile challenge between four-oared crews among local fishermen who rowed against the stream. Further interest was aroused after Cheltenham College established a boat club in 1860, later siting their boathouse at the Lower Lode, an association that continues to the present day. That same year, Frederick Moore (1832–1900), a solicitor who founded the *Tewkesbury Register and Agricultural Gazette* two years earlier, established an annual regatta, which continued until 1906. Originally scheduled to take place between the point where the Avon meets the Severn and the Mythe Bridge, the inaugural event had to be changed at the last minute because of high winds, the starting point being moved to Bushley, upstream from the Mythe Bridge.

As rowing became a more popular pursuit for amateurs Tewkesbury played an influential role in helping to define what is meant by an 'amateur', the following definition used by the Tewkesbury Regatta Committee also being adopted by the Amateur Rowing Association (ARA), now British Rowing, in 1885:

> . . . one who has never rowed for a money prize, or got his living by working on the water, or built or let out boats for hire, or knowingly competed with or against a professional (except in a scratch race previous to the year 1885), or taught or assisted in the practice of athletic exercises of any kind of profit, or been engaged in any menial duty or manual labour.

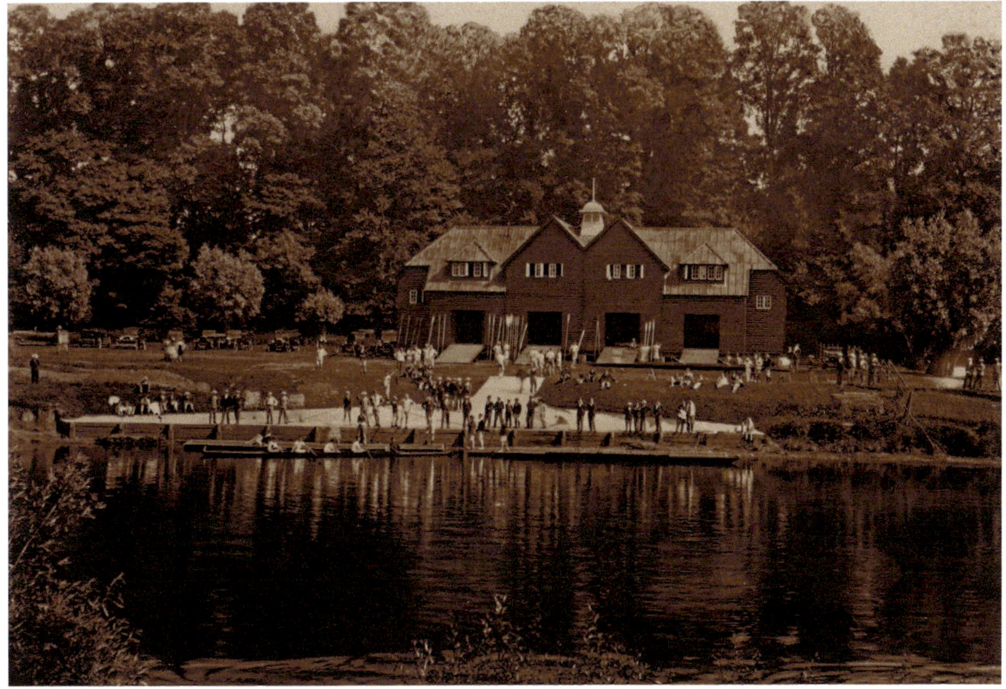

Cheltenham College Boathouse.

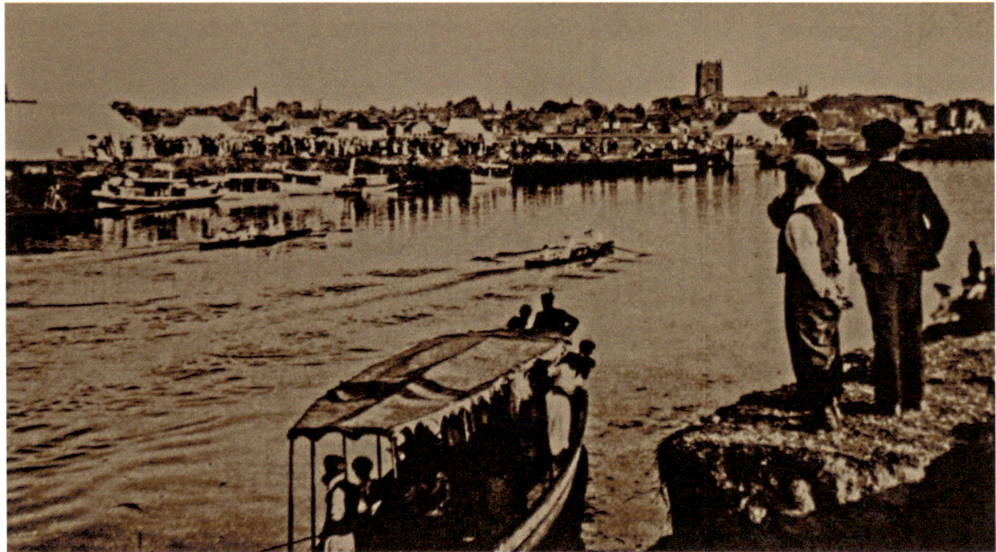

Tewkesbury Regatta, *c.* 1910.

While this appeared fairly restrictive, in a letter to *The Field,* as secretary to the Regatta, Frederick Moore commented that while certain practices might 'shock the delicate feelings of the lavender-gloved amateur' it was important that 'if rowing is to be encouraged, we must not be too thin-skinned'.

Among the most unusual rowers associated with Tewkesbury was Samuel Thomas Osborne (*c.* 1859–1905) who, for a while, became a national celebrity after becoming the first man on record to row across the English Channel. Although not born in Tewkesbury, the ex-Mercantile Marine seaman lived there for some time, working as a carpenter for the builders Messrs Collins and Godfrey, who employed his uncle, William Watts, as a foreman, while his sister, Mary Martin, resided at No. 103 High Street. He first came to prominence locally on Easter Monday 1886 after sculling an outrigger boat on the Severn and Berkeley Canal, completing the 50-mile journey from Tewkesbury to Sharpness Point in around ten hours. Impressed by the accomplishment of this local amateur the *Tewkesbury Register* hoped it would henceforth 'encourage others to take up rowing practice generally' despite the lamentable underutilisation of the town's excellent facilities for practice. Just over two years later, on 22 May 1888, Osborne achieved an even more remarkable feat, summarised in the following telegram he sent from France:

> Samuel Osborne, of Tewkesbury, Gloucestershire, left Dover yesterday, 11 a.m., arrived at 12.30 this (Tuesday) afternoon, two miles from Boulogne. No provisions or compass. Osborne good condition, and returns to-night per South-Eastern Railway boat.

Reported widely in local newspapers across the country, from Aberdeen to York, and even in the foreign press, some articles reproduced his portrait as an engraving, taken from a photograph by the Tewkesbury photographer Ernest A. Brown, who had a studio at No. 37

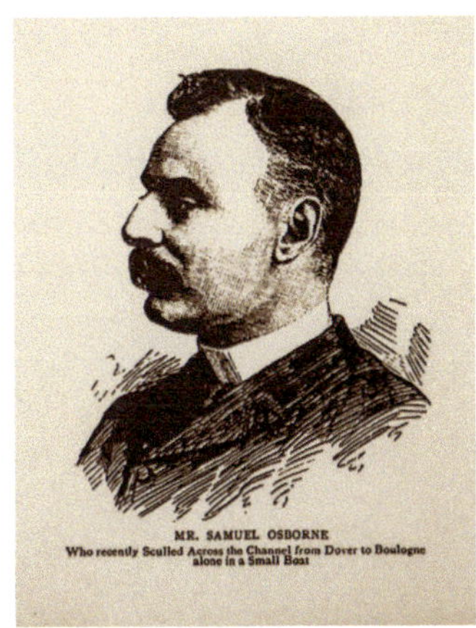

Samuel Thomas Osborne.

High Street. Said to resemble the Channel swimmer Captain Matthew Webb (1848–83) in appearance, Osborne was feted as a hero. While his stated aim had been to prove that a single man could row across the Channel, and thereby demonstrate that recent crossings made, for example, by Oxford University's eight-man crew supported by a steamer was 'no great feat of endurance', some commentators criticised it as a foolhardy, irresponsible stunt given that he lied about his real intentions after hiring the boat in Dover. Anxiety for his safety had been raised and the boat's owner feared for his vessel's return. Nevertheless, this did not dampen the spirits of the celebratory dinner in his honour chaired by Frederick Moore at the Anchor Hotel when he returned to Tewkesbury. Later, in October 1888, Osborne tried his hand as an inventor when he tested his design for a life-saving raft, measuring 22 feet by 9 feet 3 inches, in Bristol's floating harbour. Intending then to tow his raft up the Severn to exhibit it at Tewkesbury Regatta before attempting to cross St George's Channel to Ireland, Osborne suffered an accident on the way, delaying his arrival at Lower Lode to 7 o'clock the following evening. Despite this, his raft was put on display in the Quay Pit, near Quay Bridge, but he never made the journey to Ireland. Thereafter, it appears Osborne provided fundraising support for the Conservative Party at the Tewkesbury Regatta on 9 August 1890 before, later, moving to Painswick and then London where he died from heart disease at a relatively young age.

DID YOU KNOW?
Among the town's long-forgotten pastimes is the game of quoits. In 1800, when it was played in a spacious yard at the Upper Lode, the game attracted large numbers of contestants and spectators throughout England. Tewkesbury produced some accomplished players, including Henry White, a landlord, who became the finest player in Gloucestershire after winning significant prize money against another highly regarded player in a two-legged contest that took place in August 1843 at the Ram Inn, Gloucester, and the Lower Lode Inn.

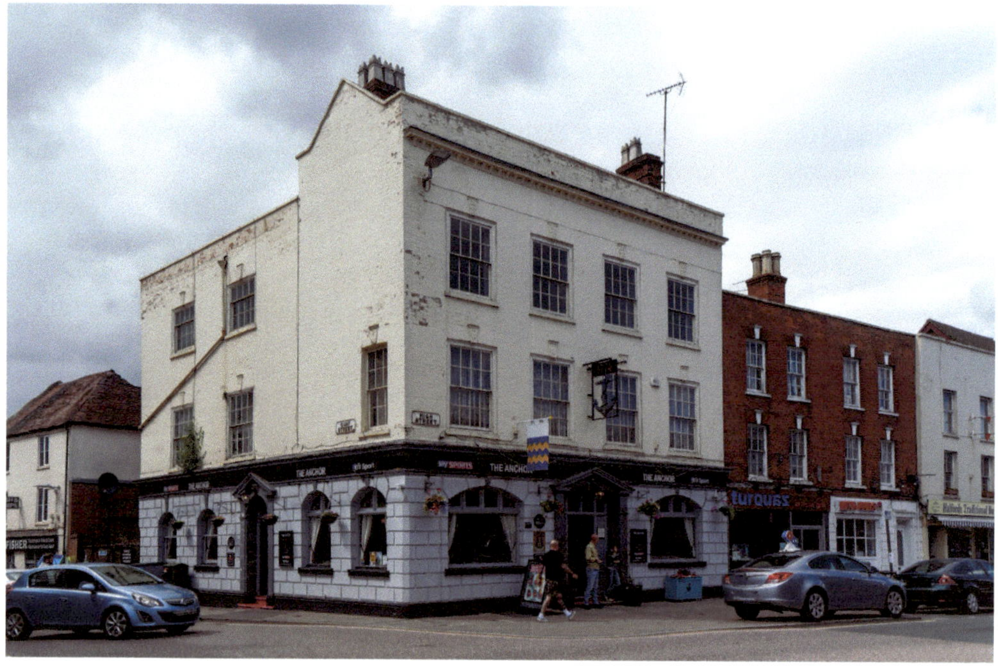

The Anchor (at No. 42 High Street) today.

Cricket

The earliest recorded game of Tewkesbury Cricket Club took place on 11 July 1842 when a friendly game was played on Bushley Common against the Cheltenham and Prestbury club. Although the weather was not kind, the *Hereford Times* commenting that 'wet boots and wet jackets would have served to damp the ardour of less spirited knights of the bat', the Tewkesburians emerged triumphant, helped in part by some skilful bowling from Mr Chandler and precision fielding from Mr Phelps at long stop, who ensured no byes were scored. While various grounds were used by the club in those early years, including on the Ham and in fields or meadows located near Barton Street and adjacent to Ashchurch Road, from 1869 onwards, Swilgate Meadow became the club's permanent home. Apart from the threat of flooding, which necessitated the raising of the original pavilion, firstly using wooden stilts and then brick pillars, another challenge of playing cricket there occasionally arises when play coincides with the bell ringers' practice from the neighbouring abbey. In 1966, John Moore observed: 'Even if you yelled "Howzat!" at the top of your voice the umpire had to shake his head, because he couldn't hear you.' Among the more unusual games played at Swilgate was a fifty-over match between Lancashire and Yorkshire held on 21 July 1971, the first time this fixture has been held outside their counties. Arranged as part of the quincentenary anniversary celebrations of the Battle of Tewkesbury, on this occasion the 'War of the Roses' resulted in victory for the House of Lancaster by a single run.

Among the famous players associated with the club is Cheltenham-born Gilbert Jessop, who first played for Tewkesbury in 1893. Although probably best remembered as a

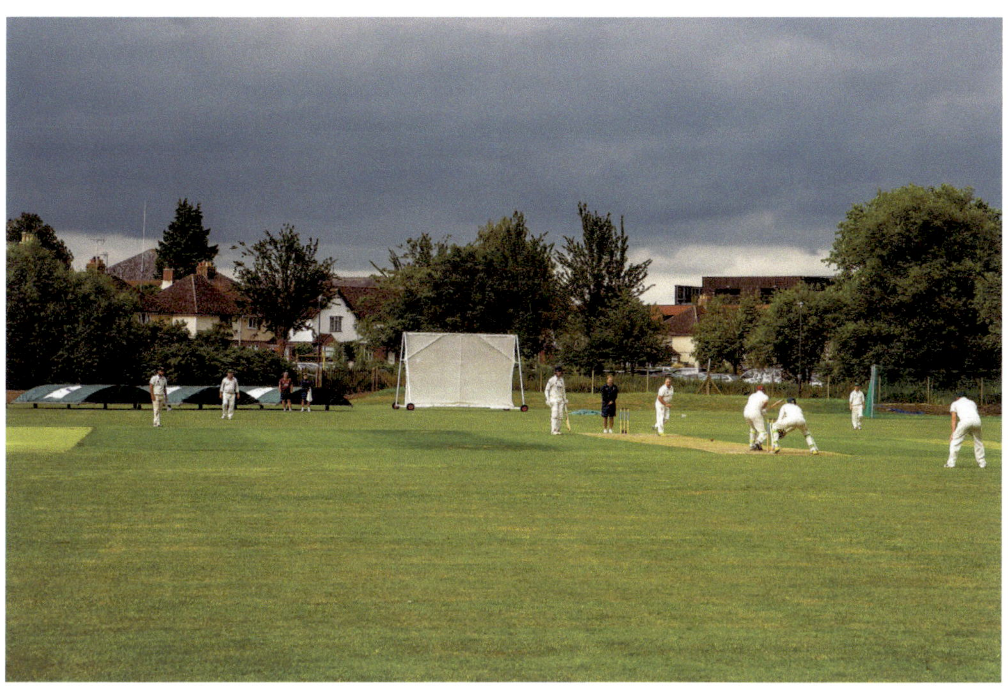

Above: The ground at Swilgate Meadow today.

Right: Gilbert Jessop.

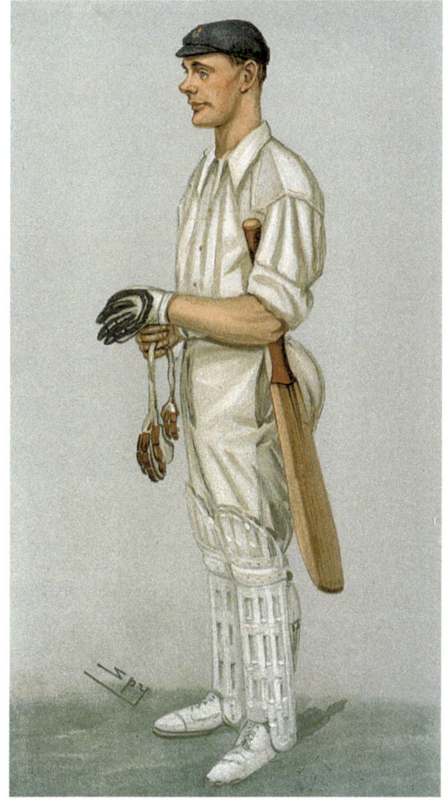

big-hitter who once smashed a ball through the pavilion's window, Jessop also excelled as a bowler: playing against Evesham in August 1896, his bowling display saw him take 7 wickets for just 13 runs, during which he even succeeded in breaking one of the stumps into pieces! On another occasion at Tewkesbury, when Jessop was at the height of his success, he commented on his appreciation of the quality of the pitch 'by remarking that he wished he could take it about with him in his bag'.

Swimming

Given Tewkesbury's situation on the confluence of two major rivers, the Severn and Avon, water has always played a major part in the town's development. While it has presented many risks and dangers, most notably flooding and drowning (accidental or otherwise), river water has also yielded opportunities for leisure and sport. The earliest reference to providing a swimming bath in Tewkesbury came between 1862 and 1868 when the industrial boatbuilder Bathurst announced the availability of a swimming pool, in addition to pleasure craft. Located between the two rivers at Stanchard Pit, the pool formed the subject of a satirical cartoon in the early 1930s when the local swimming club moved its headquarters there. Despite the danger of slipping into the river from the clayey bank here, this facility enabled youngsters to learn to swim and tamed a black spot for drowning.

Although Stanchard Pit became popular the need to pay for admission reduced its appeal, the *Cheltenham Chronicle* commenting that 'the majority of Tewkesbury folk prefer to undress and dress on the river bank rather than pay a subscription'. For this reason, during this time, a site at Sandy Point on the River Severn, opposite the Upper Lode Locks, attracted larger numbers of bathers. Here, many locals, seemingly unaware of the nearby council refuse tip located in former withy beds, fondly remembered Sid Walkley, son of a local councillor, regularly replenishing the site with sand.

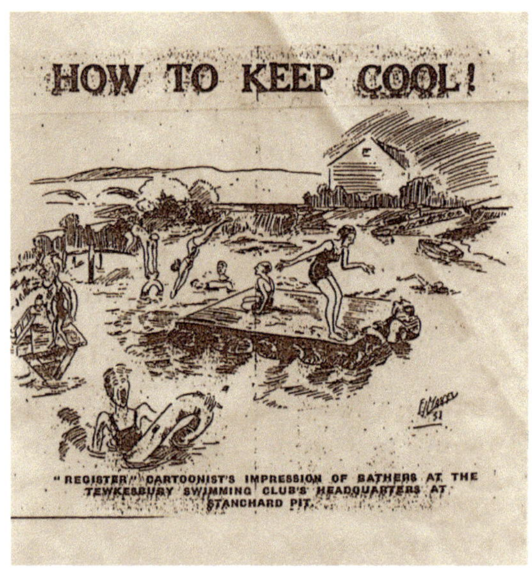

The Swimming Club at Stanchard Pit, 1933.

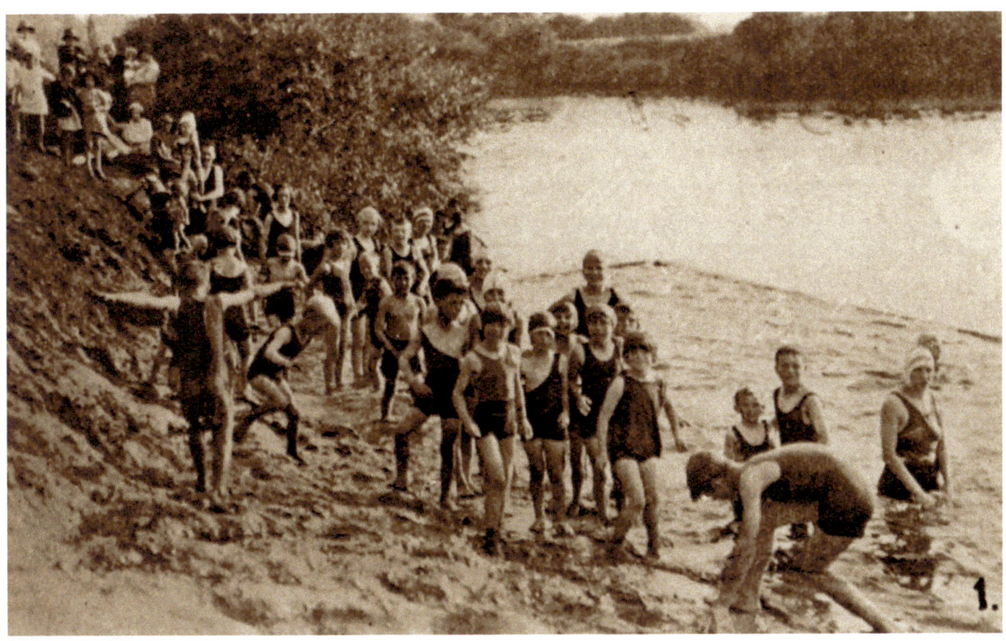

Children playing at Sandy Point, *c.* 1930.

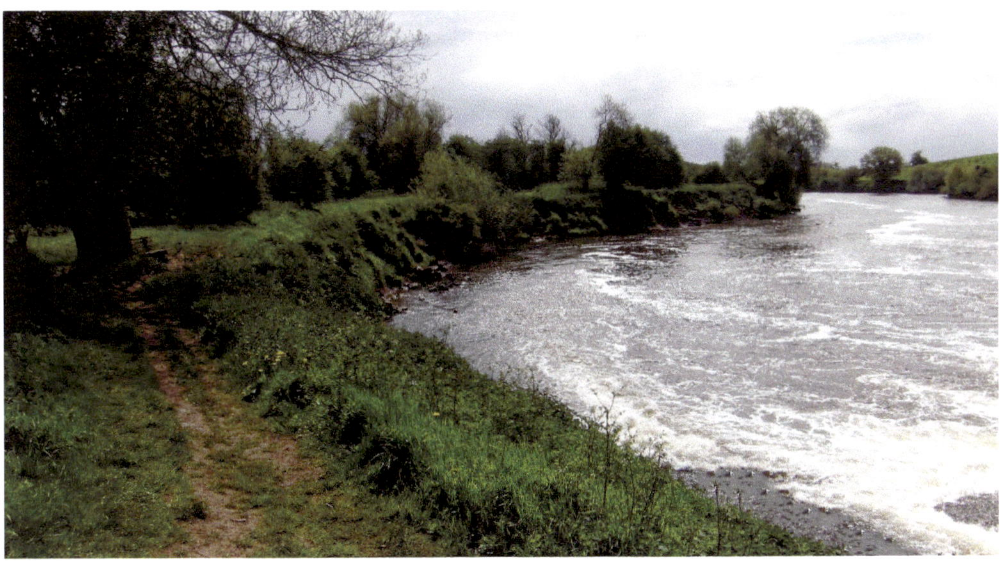

Sandy Point, looking deserted in 2013.

Another favourite swimming place, known as the '32', though the origin of its name remains a mystery, was located on the Mill Avon on the town side of the Abbey Mills. In 1952, as support increased to construct an outdoor swimming pool, the town's authorities were faced with a dilemma: to fund the latter or renovate the derelict banks of the Mill

Avon through creating a riverside walk. Nevertheless, the drowning of two small children around this time forced the decision in favour of a pool, leading to the construction of the Tewkesbury Lido, infamously known as the 'Bird Bath', on the site of what is now Marquis Motorhomes, behind the Gloucester Road coach park and toilets. However, its small size, coupled with the cold water and inadequate changing facilities, reduced its overall attractiveness. Much greater success was achieved with the much-loved Cascades Swimming Pool. Opened in time for Queen Elizabeth II's historic visit to Tewkesbury in 1971, it provided warmth and the high-quality facilities that the town desired. Despite its success, in 2013, the District Council controversially replaced this pool with a new purpose-built leisure centre on its headquarters' site. Although an unpopular decision, at least the town still provides a pool for local children to learn to swim and avoid the risk of drowning in Tewkesbury's rivers.

Flying Exhibition

Among the unusual exhibitions, which took place in the town in the early twentieth century, were flying exhibitions in a 50-horsepower Bleriot monoplane by the celebrated aviator Gustav Hamel (1889–1914). Due to take place from 3 o'clock on 23 October 1913 at Windmill Hill – site of the bloody meadow and, earlier, a Bronze Age settlement and now the site of the Borough Council Offices – the Hamburg-born pilot arrived half-an-hour early after departing from Upton-upon-Severn and mistakenly turning right instead of left at the River Avon, intending originally to visit Pershore first. Nevertheless, a large crowd had already gathered, encouraged no doubt by the advert in the *Tewkesbury Register* promising the opportunity to witness 'the beauty and grace of flying' and thrilling

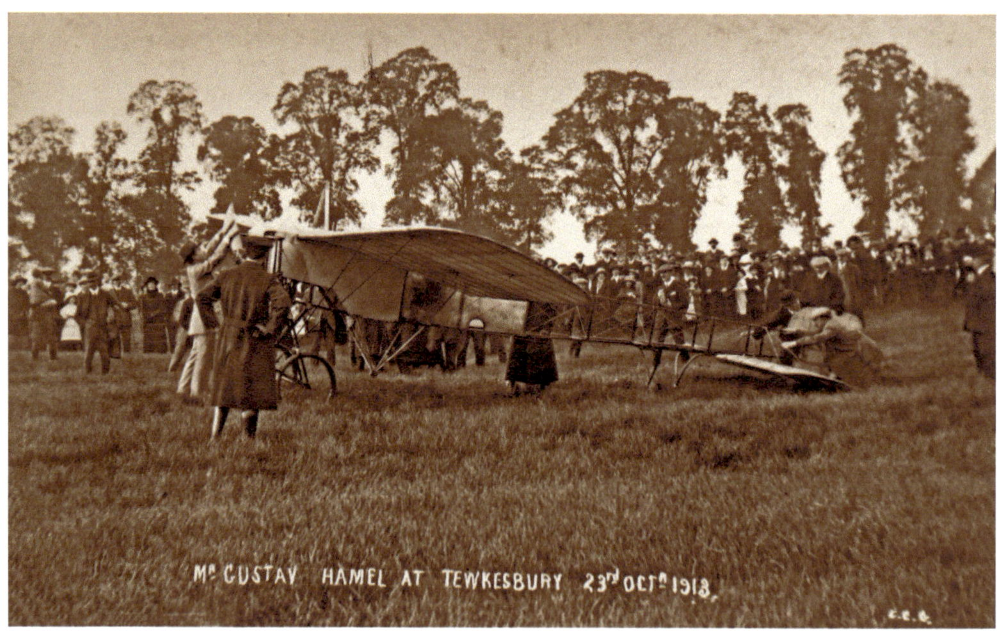

Postcard celebrating Gustav Hamel's exhibition flights.

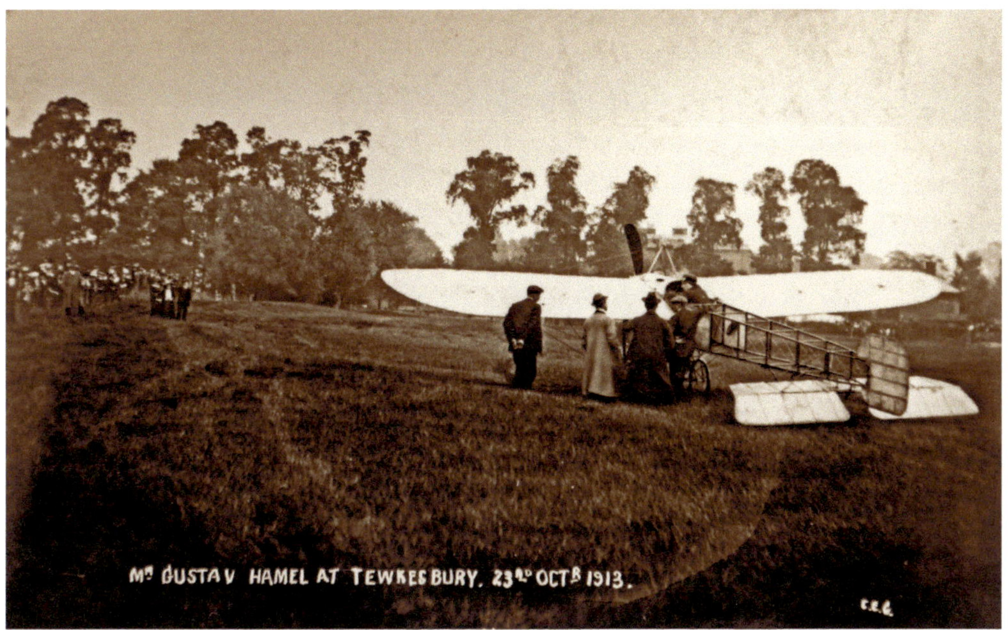

Another postcard celebrating Hamel's historic flight.

displays of banking, volplanes and pancake descents. Keen to fulfil his commitment at Pershore, however, Hamel immediately flew north to the neighbouring town, reappearing forty-five minutes later above Tewkesbury Abbey at a height of around 800 feet before executing a graceful volplane and spiral descent. A 500-strong crowd, who bought tickets for 1s 6d (half price for under-12s), gave him a rapturous welcome. Renowned for having previously made the first official airmail flight in the country and other records, including the first cross-channel return flight and the first flight from England to Germany, involving the crossing of five frontiers, Hamel continued with an exhibition of banking and gliding before alighting on the Ham. Then, much to the amusement of the spectators, he flew low over the Ham's broad acres, rounding up the cattle and frightening some boys, two of whom, according to the *Register*, 'flung themselves on the grass, whilst their companions took to their heels'. Thereafter, Hamel made two more flights from the Ham, including one in the direction of the Mythe before landing at Tewkesbury Park. Although originally planning to leave his plane in a hangar at Upton that evening, given the fading light, he decided instead to house it overnight in Tewkesbury. Therefore, it was dismantled and taken to the Tewkesbury Garage (once located at Nos 31–32 High Street, the site now occupied by Poundland) for later transfer. While this was Hamel's only appearance in Tewkesbury, the townsfolk continued to follow his career with interest, less than three months later, the *Register* reporting that Hamel had achieved the distinction of being the first aviator to loop the loop with a lady passenger. Sadly, on 30 May 1914, it also expressed fear of the intrepid aviator's demise after he disappeared during a cross-channel flight, a few days before announcing his intention to attempt to fly across the Atlantic.

DID YOU KNOW?

While the rivers have generally only provided Tewkesbury with opportunities for fair weather swimming, during some of the country's severest winters they have also enabled participation in winter sports. In January 1963, for example, the Avon was frozen to a depth of 6 inches at the Abbey Mill – the first time since 1947 – making the possibility of ice skating and ice hockey feasible. One impromptu ice hockey match took place near King John's bridge, utilising walking sticks and a tin can.

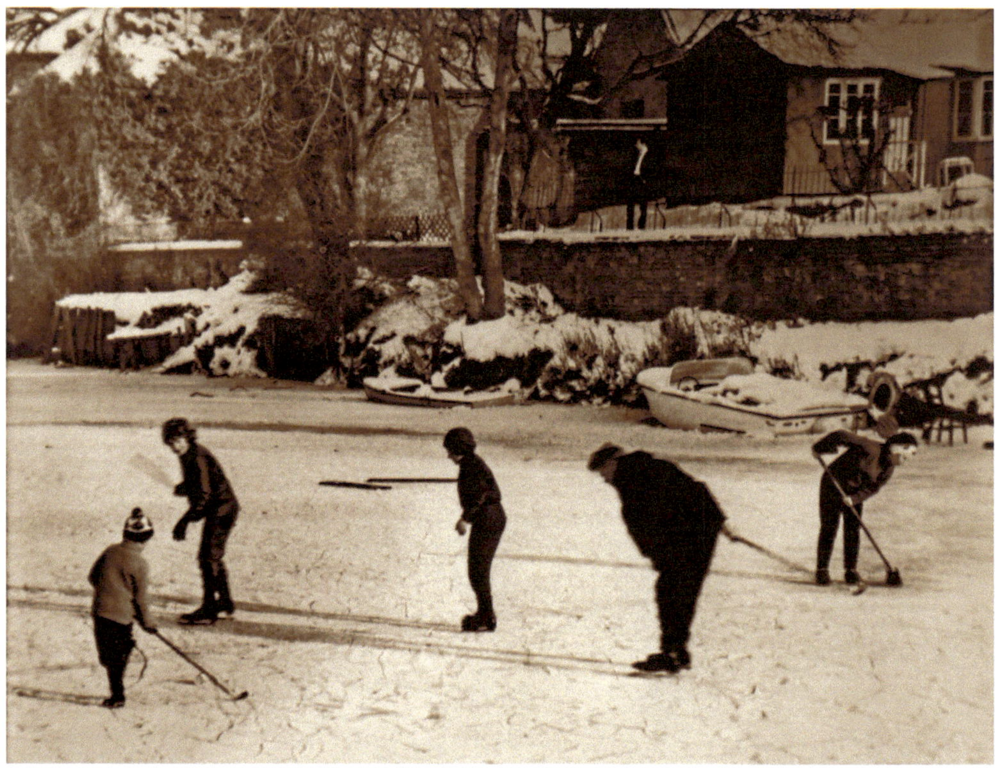

The impromptu ice hockey match near King John's Bridge.

7. Literary Connections

Tewkesbury has been immortalised as a place in Mrs Craik's novel *John Halifax, Gentleman* (1865) and the writings of John Moore (1907–67) – having been fictionalised as Norton Bury and Elmbury respectively. The town, however, has also inspired a wide range of other writers. While some of their creativity has been stimulated through the Battle of Tewkesbury, others have found expression through the town's buildings, culinary traditions and geographic features.

William Shakespeare (1564–1616)

Given Stratford-upon-Avon's proximity to Tewkesbury, Shakespeare would undoubtedly have been acquainted with the town. While some have claimed that he performed, as an actor with a travelling troupe, at Ye Olde Black Bear Inn, High Street, in the sixteenth century, it has never been reliably recorded. However, his history plays, including those referring to the Battle of Tewkesbury, have made a significant impact on how historical events and characters have been interpreted. In particular, they have helped to establish the 'Tudor Myth' of the Wars of the Roses in the national consciousness through portraying a century of civil war and strife, which began with the unlawful overthrow of Richard II in 1399 and ended with the unifying force brought by Henry VII and the reconciliation between the Houses of Lancaster and York. Furthermore, Shakespeare, having been strongly influenced by the contemporary politics of Elizabethan England, memorably portrays Richard, Duke of Gloucester (later Richard III), as a murderous and

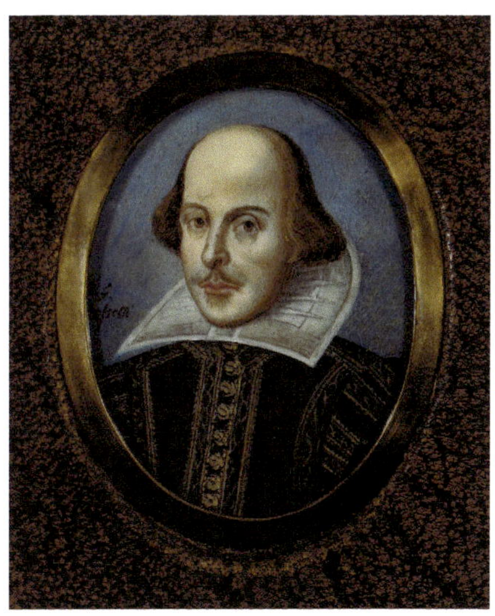

Portrait of Shakespeare, by Dante Gabriel Rossetti.

Machiavellian villain. For example, in Act I Scene II of *Richard III*, as he unscrupulously seeks to woo Margaret, despite the fact that she is still grieving the loss of both her husband and her son, Richard comments:

Hath she forgot already that brave prince; Edward, her lord, whom I, some three months since; Stabb'd in my angry mood at Tewksbury?

In the ensuing scene Margaret rejects Richard's advances and exclaims: 'Thou slewest my husband Henry in the Tower; And Edward, my poor son, at Tewksbury'. Later, in Act V Scene III, Prince Edward's ghost visits Richard on the eve of the all-important Battle of Bosworth (22 August 1485) that will ultimately decide Richard's fate. The ghost addresses Richard by saying: 'Let me sit heavy on thy soul to-morrow!; Think, how thou stab'dst me in my prime of youth; At Tewksbury: despair, therefore, and die!' The ghost's wish is realised the following morning when Richard, in the midst of battle, is knocked from his horse and then killed after famously pleading, 'A horse! A horse! My kingdom for a horse!'. Following Richard's death, the Earl of Richmond is proclaimed King Henry VII, thereby unifying the Houses of Lancaster and York but also reinforcing the 'Tudor Myth'.

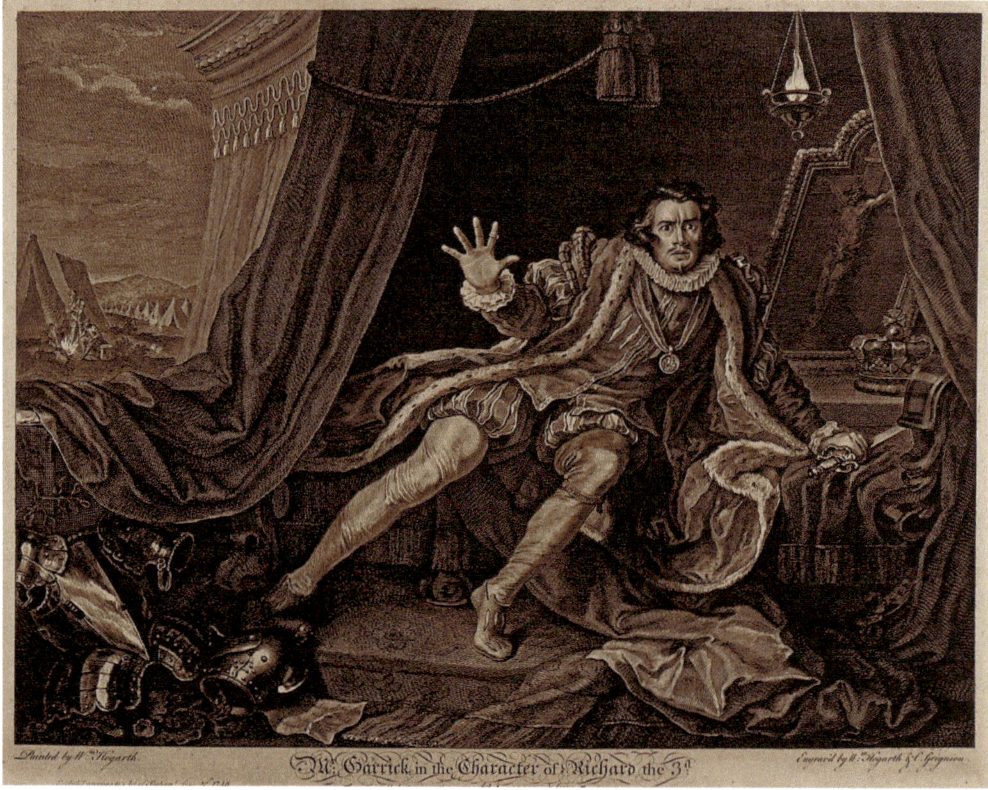

David Garrick in the role of Richard III. Etching after W. Hogarth.

Shakespeare's Descendants

Although records of the bard's visits to Tewkesbury do not exist, physical links to his family can be seen in the town today. These include the grave of Thomas Shakespear[e] Hart, which can be found near the entrance to the old Baptist Chapel burial ground. Although William Shakespeare's line of direct descendants ceased in 1670, that of his sister, Joan Shakespeare (1569–1646), who married William Hart, continues to the present day. Through this line a Tewkesbury connection began through John Hart (1755–1800), a sixth descendant from the poet, whose grave can be found on the north side of the abbey.

Interestingly, in 1834, James Bennett also recorded a meeting that took place between the editor of the *Monthly Magazine* and one of William Shakespeare's relatives William Shakspeare Hart [sic], who was a chair maker and journeyman by trade. William Shakespeare Hart (1778–1834) was one of John Hart's three children. He used to put a 5-feet-long walking-stick on display, which he claimed to have once belonged to William Shakespeare. Furthermore, according to the editor, the contour of his face closely resembled the bard's portrait used in the first folio edition of his plays. While living in relative poverty with his wife and five children, it was said he never benefitted from the Shakespeare name, having to endure instead incessant teasing by Tewkesburians because of it. Nevertheless, following the interview he was given a guinea by the editor.

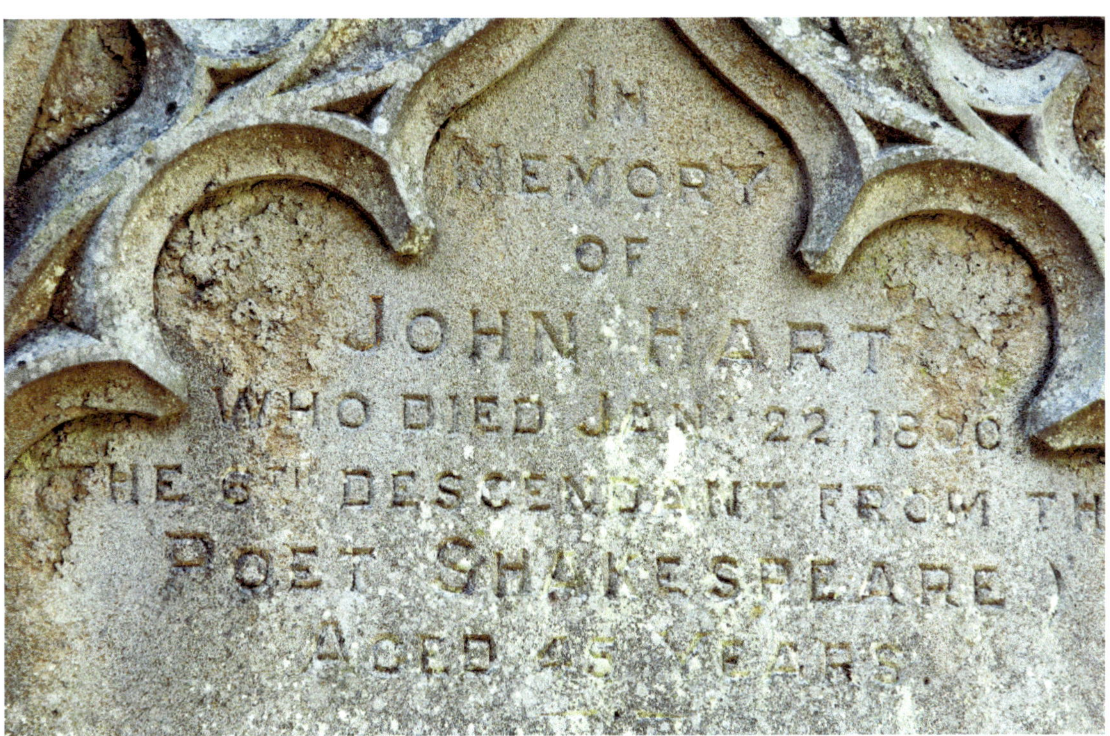

Gravestone of John Hart.

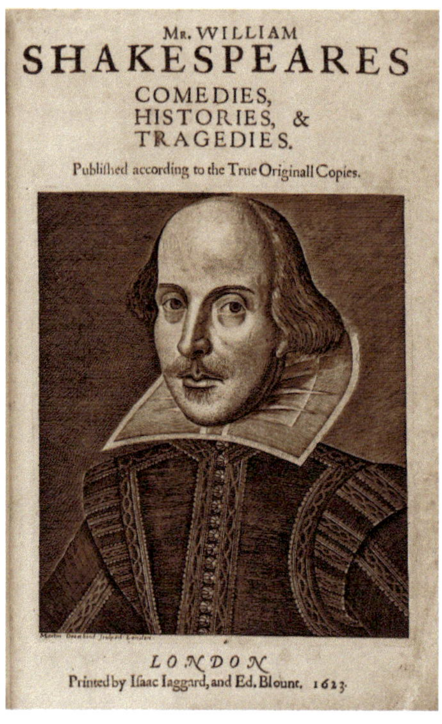

The first folio edition.

John Taylor (1578–1653)

Among the writers who wrote about Tewkesbury's riverine situation is Gloucester-born John Taylor, a ferryman who dubbed himself as the 'Water Poet'. Keen to promote the trading advantages offered by river transport he often undertook daring and whimsical journeys, on one occasion even attempting (unsuccessfully) to row down the Thames in a boat made from paper, using large fish tied to canes as oars. He then recorded these adventurous voyages in doggerel verse. In 1641, while he recorded various journeys through Tewkesbury, rather than using them as publicity stunts his aim was more

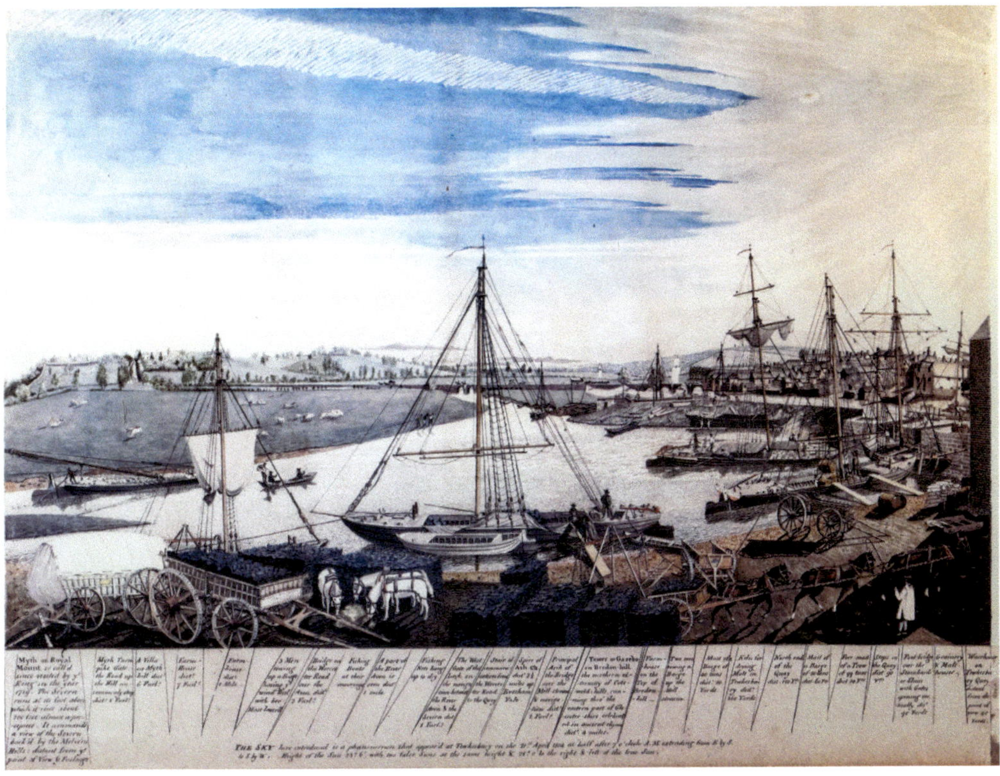

Tewkesbury Quay on 21 April 1804 by an unknown artist.

straightforward: to show how easy it was to travel from Gloucester along the Severn and join the Avon at Tewkesbury. He wrote:

> And on Munday the 30. August I past up Severne, by Glocester (and working all night) came in the morning betimes to Tewxbury, into another River called Avon, which by the great charge and industry of Master Sands is made navigable, many miles up into the Countrey.

Cecilia Cooper (1799–1863)

Among the more unusual writers who lived in Tewkesbury was Cecilia Cooper, an obscure, minor Romantic poet. Working as a school mistress she lived, for a while, in Lilley's Alley with family relatives. According to research undertaken by Steve Goodchild it seems likely that the family suffered a loss in status when her father, previously a carpet manufacturer in Kidderminster, became insolvent and moved the family to a humbler existence in Tewkesbury – he as a dyer and his daughters trying their hand at running dame schools, an attempt at retaining their middle-class status. It is likely that Cooper was living in Lilley's Alley when she wrote her forty-six-page poem 'The Battle of Tewkesbury' (1820) since, in the preface, she comments that her 'residence command[s] a View of the Intrenchments of Queen Margaret, and the Ground on which this dreadful conflict took

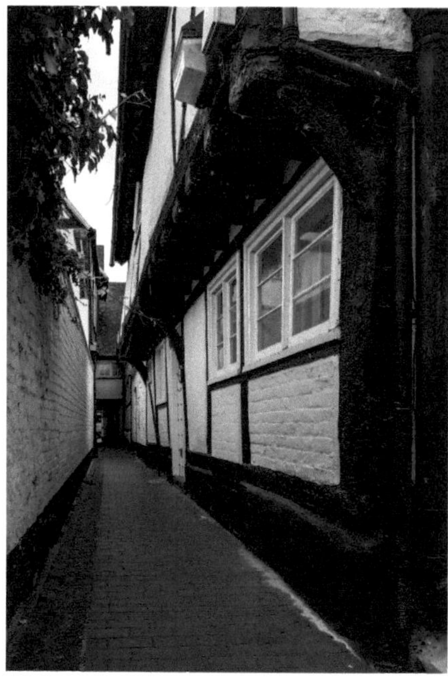

Lilley's Lane.

place.' From the rear side of the alley she would have looked south-westwards towards the Vineyards where a monument to the battle is located today.

On the surface the poem appears to be a straightforward evocation of scenes from the battle. Nevertheless, there are several clues which reveal Cooper's real intent behind the poem. The first is the poem's formal dedication to the local aristocratic MPs for Tewkesbury, J. E. Dowdeswell, and John Martin. Cooper clearly knew both as not only do they appear in the book's list of subscribers but also in the way that she expresses her personal gratitude towards them. The second clue comes from the preface, which expresses the poem's clear intention, that 'persons of every rank, even of the lowest condition in life, may learn to bear their own difficulties and misfortunes with greater patience and resignation, when they see to what extreme distresses, even the most noble and the great, are likewise subject.' Cooper clearly had pretentions, and many of her allegories in the poem about the fall of the mighty may well be a rueful reflection on her own circumstances. Her humble position is perhaps emphasised when she states that 'among all sufferers, none feel their misfortunes more keenly than those who have been most indebted to Fortune for the distinctions of high birth'. Her didactic intent with the poem is further illustrated when she adds that 'Some illustrious examples of these truths may be found in the following Poem, The Battle of Tewkesbury'. It is also interesting to note how self-deprecating Cooper appears when explaining that as 'a young and unlettered female' she may be thought to be 'presumptuous ... in, attempting to write on so great an Historical Event'. However, the wealth of detailed historical references Cooper cites in this poem, including, for example, Holinshed's *Chronicles of England, Scotland and Ireland*, David Hume's *History of England*, Michel Baudier's *History of Margaret of Anjou*, and the *Chronicle of Tewkesbury Abbey* suggests that she was a well-educated person.

Cooper also reveals her willingness to take sides between the Houses of Lancaster and York. In the poem she clearly favours the Lancastrian cause and, in accordance with the popular Lancastrian myth of the day, she presents Margaret of Anjou as an English Joan of Arc-type figure. However, of even greater interest are the concluding lines to the poem, which reveal the real message that Cooper wishes to convey, pledging her political allegiance to the legacy of King George III, who died three months before the poem was written:

The bloody Quarrels of these Houses show; What horrid scenes from Civil Discord flow; May no contending Parties, here, again; Stain this fair Land with blood of Subjects slain; But, may the Subjects' Love the Throne secure; To Brunswick's Line 'till Time shall be no more; The lengthen'd reign of George the Third, has prov'd; A Monarch's Safeguard is – his People's Love!'

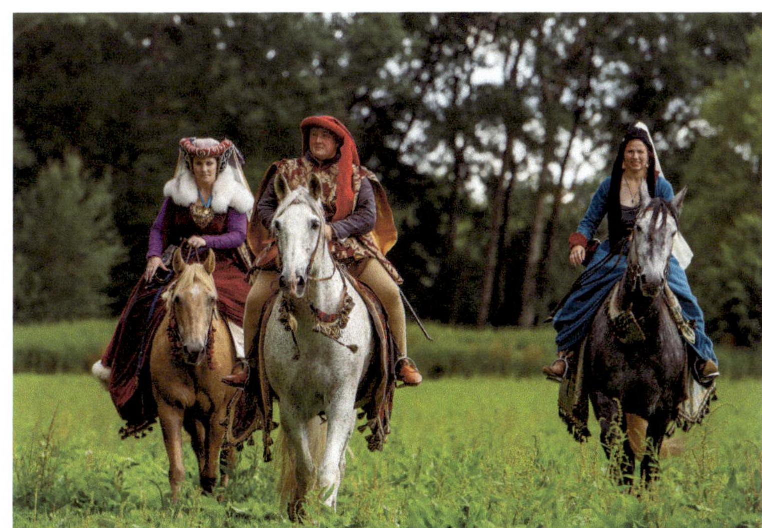

550th anniversary of Margaret of Anjou's ride to Tewkesbury, 1 May 2021.

Herman Melville (1819-1891)

Among the more obscure literary connections is Herman Melville (1819–91), best known for his novel *Moby-Dick* (1851). In 1863, while visiting Oxford, he was impressed by the beauty and tranquillity of the cloisters, which, he wrote, were a far cry from 'all the violence of revolutions'. It was there that he wrote a poem comparing the 1862 American Civil War battle, fought between Union and Confederate army forces, with the Wars of the Roses. By referring to the Battle of Tewkesbury in the poem Melville highlighted the dangers of fratricidal strife and the fact that history was now repeating itself on the other side of the Atlantic. The last few lines of his poem read:

> Monks blessed the fratricidal lance; And sisters scarfs could twine; Do North and South the sin retain; Of Yorkist and Lancastrian?

Charles Dickens (1812–70)

One of the town's buildings, which has been greatly celebrated through literature, is the Royal Hop Pole in Church Street. An amalgamation of buildings dating from the fifteenth and eighteenth centuries the inn, originally known as the Hop Pole, received its 'Royal' prefix in the 1890s, following a visit from the impecunious parents of 'Princess May', later Queen Mary, royal consort of George V. However, it was while the inn served as a major coaching inn that Charles Dickens first became acquainted with the Hop Pole, lodging there whilst working as a reporter. Later, from 1836 to 1837, drawing on this experience, he published his first novel in serial form as *The Posthumous Papers of the Pickwick Club*. Well aware that the days of stagecoach travel were numbered, given the advent of railways, Dickens sets *Pickwick Papers* in the late 1820s, the charm of the journey made by Samuel Pickwick and his fellow travellers conjuring up the atmosphere of what would soon become a lost age. As the final stop in the Pickwick Club's journey between Bristol and Birmingham the Hop Pole became the ideal location for Dickens to immortalise it as the place where they consumed considerable quantities of ale, Madeira and port, after which 'Bob and Mr. Weller sang duets in the dickey'. The visit, complete with a stagecoach – and a highway man – was commemorated on its centenary in 1828 by the then thriving Dickens Society (see p. 58).

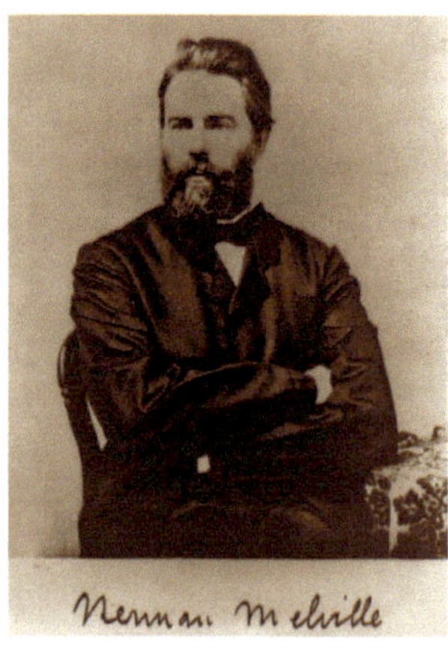

Herman Melville, *c.* 1860.

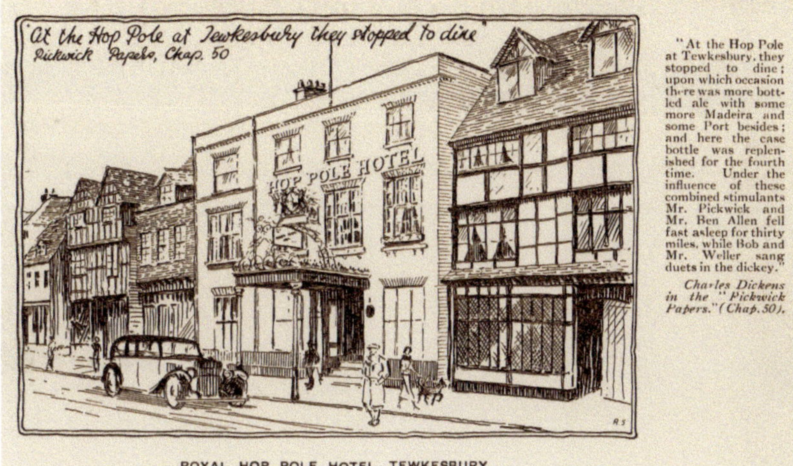

Postcard celebrating the inn's association with Dickens.

Ivor Gurney (1890–1937)

During the First World War Ivor Gurney served in the Gloucester Regiment on the Western Front between 1915 and 1917. Later, he reflected on how the experience of war crystallised his calling as a poet: 'As of Cotswold: war told me: I was elect, I was born fit; To praise the three hundred feet depth of every acre; Between Tewkesbury and Stroudway...' However, the experience of war also contributed to a deterioration in his mental health and he was committed to a mental hospital from 1922. It was during this troubled period of his life that he wrote three poems about Tewkesbury, one of which, simply called 'Tewkesbury', encapsulates much of its history and features.

In 1926, the poet also wrote a five-act play called *The Tewkesbury Trial*. Set in various locations within Tewkesbury, as well as around Gloucestershire, the Cotswolds, Warwick and (briefly) Chartres in the 1420s–30s, this work is interesting not only for some fine tavern scenes, including one set in Tewkesbury, but also for conveying some of Gurney's thoughts and ideas on landscape, music, poetry, and drama. It is possible that Gurney used poetic licence when he set one of the scenes in the reception hall of Tewkesbury Tower, unless the tower in question perhaps referred to the large embattled quadrangular building which was once used as the abbey's bell tower and later as the local gaol.

DID YOU KNOW?

The poet and writer Sir John Betjeman (1906–84) composed and read 'Inland Waterway' at the reopening of the Upper Avon Navigation on 1 June 1974. As Vice-President of the Inland Waterways Association (IWA) from 1966 to 1984 Betjeman took an active interest in the IWA. The poem has also been put to music by Tewkesbury teacher, Ben Sawyer of The Songmen ensemble.

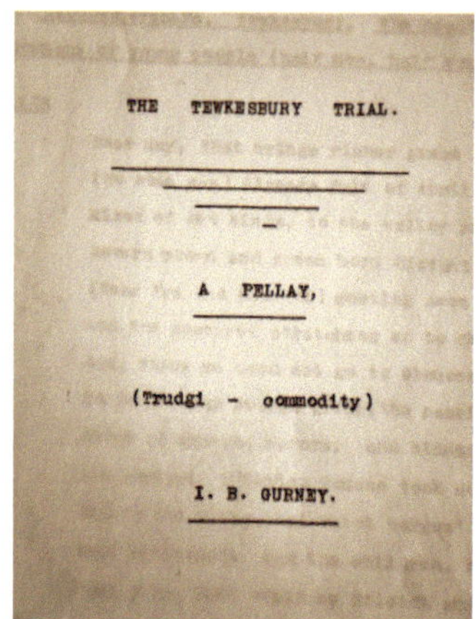

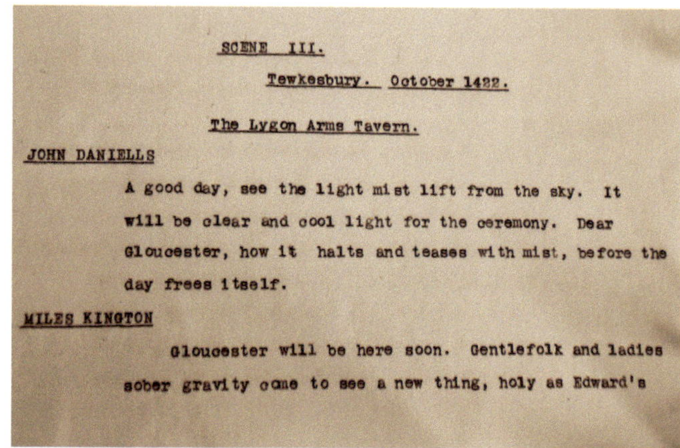

Above left: The title page from *The Tewkesbury Trial*.

Above right: Extract from one of the Tewkesbury scenes.

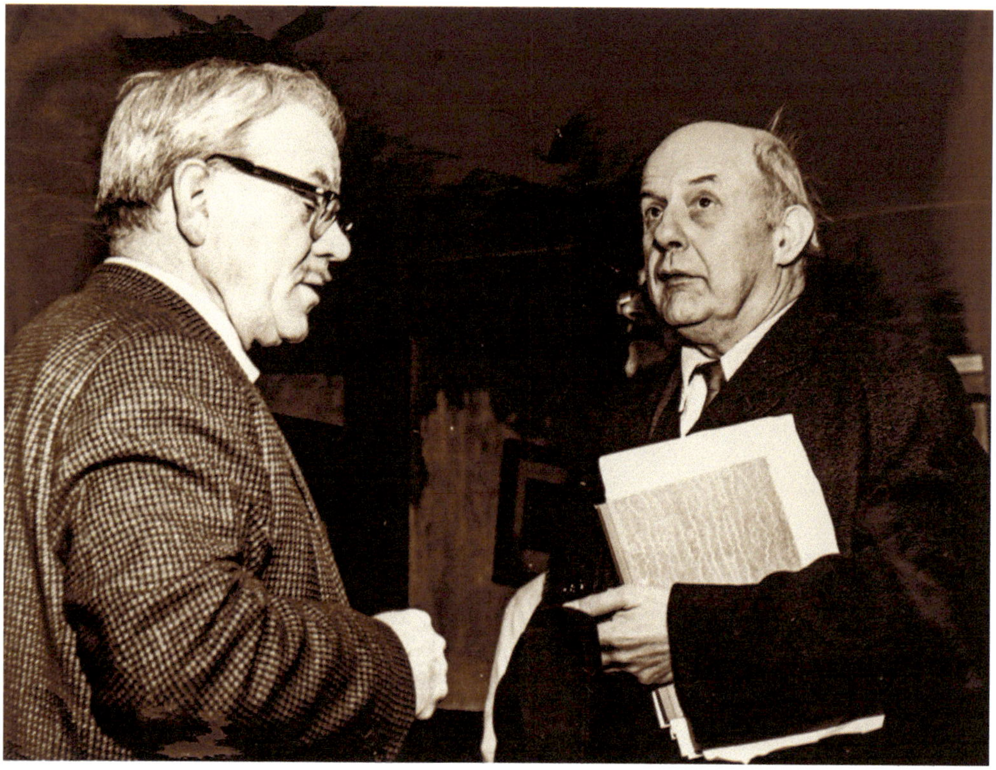

Sir John Betjeman (on the right).

8. Curiosities

In such a unique and interesting place as Tewkesbury there is a wealth of unusual and unexpected objects and associations which reveal new dimensions of the town's history – from the abbey's fascinating misericords to a 'heroic' Siberian dog which exercised daily on the Ham after surviving the trials and tribulations of life in the Antarctic and the army.

Depictions of Everyday Life

Curiously, although in line with common practice, many of the misericords found in Tewkesbury Abbey, dating from the fourteenth and fifteenth centuries, depict not only mythical and fantastic creatures but also scenes from everyday life. Among these, on the south side, west of the choir screen, are three carvings, one of which shows a cock and hen, the latter pecking from a dish. Another portrays a naked human figure with its backside exposed in a gesture of contempt, having just made a fart. Scatological subjects were often used in medieval misericords, with farting commonly associated with the devil and the hell-like stink of sulphur. Among the other misericords, located within the choir stalls, is a scene of a domestic brawl. Here, a wife holds her husband by the hair and uses a washing paddle – a wooden tool normally used to beat wet clothes – to thrash him. Another interesting carving shows a sickbed scene, with a bag of money being handed over to a doctor in payment for a promised cure. Thought to date from the mid-fourteenth century, either just prior or during the time of the Black Death, this carving possibly served as a commentary on the corrupt practices of physicians of the day. Incidentally, the Tewkesbury example, together with the equivalent scene depicted at the priory at Great Malvern, are reputedly the only two examples of its kind in England that portray the doctor as a man rather than an ape. Whether it is mermaids, griffins or the human condition, the abbey's surviving misericord carvings continue to tell some thought-provoking stories, characterised at times with a strong subversive spirit.

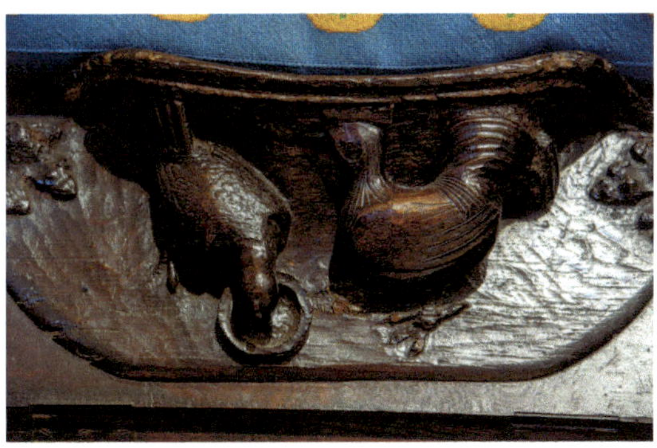

The cock and hen misericord.

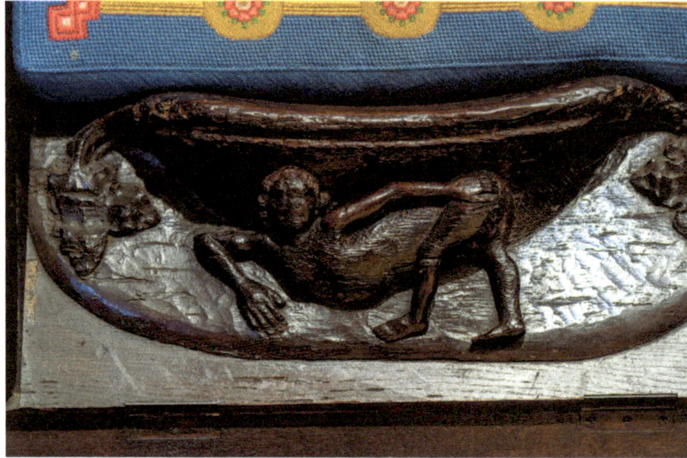

The example of the scatological subject.

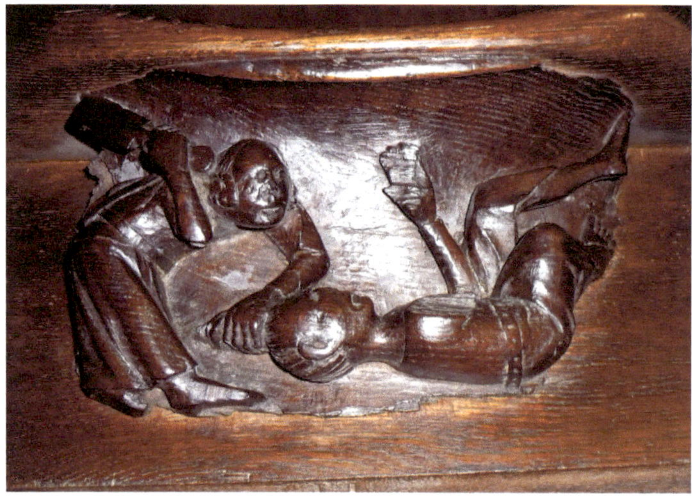

The domestic brawl.

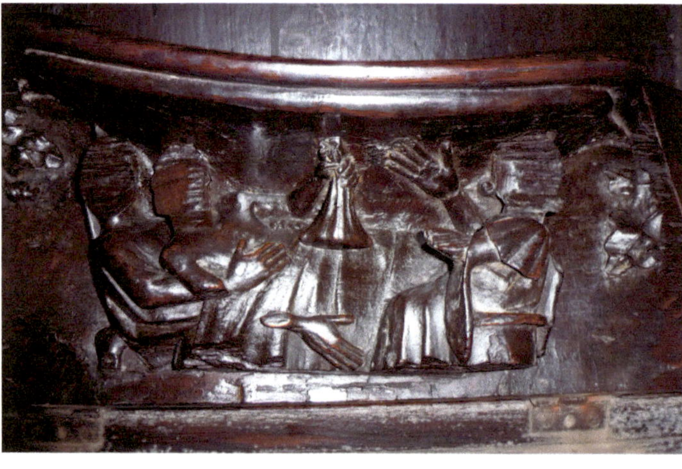

The sickbed scene.

The Decomposing Corpse

Among the most eye-catching tombs in the abbey is the Wakeman cenotaph, at the east end of the church, which commemorates John Wakeman (d. 1549), the last abbot of Tewkesbury, although this attribution is disputed. Originally intended to show two contrasting likenesses of the cleric – one living and the other dead – the double-decker alabaster monument never included the second image of the abbot dressed in fine robes since, following the dissolution, he transferred to Gloucester to become its bishop. Instead, the tomb became one of the most unusual examples of a cadaver tomb, depicting Wakeman's decaying skeleton either covered or devoured by five different types of vermin – a worm, a snake, a toad, a mouse and a snail. The cadaver effigy would originally have been placed in the lower recess, behind the openwork stone screen below, with the likeness of the abbot to be placed on the upper slab, had he died in Tewkesbury. With each animal probably generally representing the corruption of the flesh, the memorial served an important purpose: more than just a simple *memento mori*, its message was further elaborated by the symbols contained on the screen beneath the figure, which imply that to gain salvation one must follow the path of prayer and the sacrifice of Christ's Passion. Finally, the graffiti on the tomb, some of which dates from the seventeenth century, shows the early interest and popularity of this memorial. The location of the bishop's actual burial is still not known.

Concealed Shoes

Perhaps the most unusual object found so far in a Tewkesbury house during renovation work has been a Tudor merchant's shoe. Now housed in the Gloucestershire Archives. it was discovered at No. 75 High Street when a wall was being demolished to expand

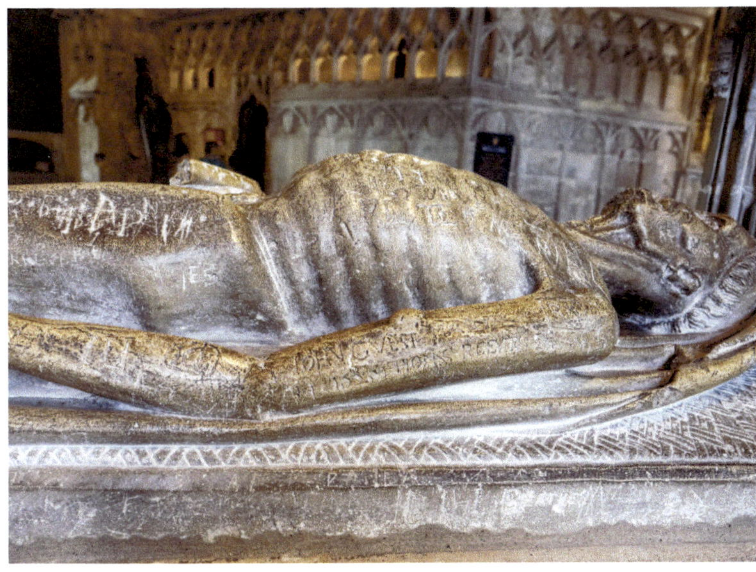

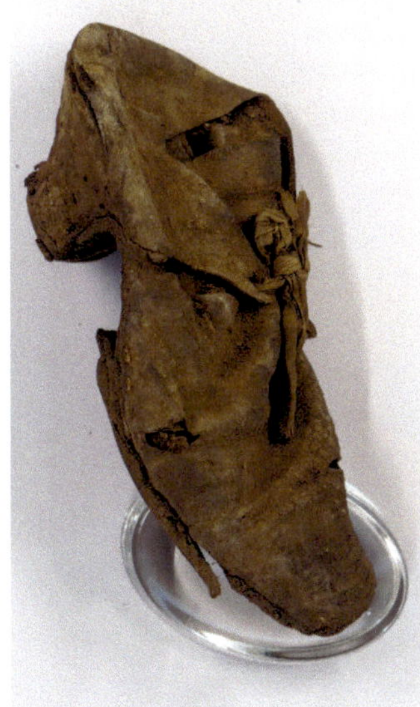

Above left: Detail from the Wakeman cenotaph.

Above right: The shoe.

the living quarters into the adjoining property. Concealed shoes are sometimes – though not commonly – discovered in British houses. One dating from 1600, which is so well preserved that its ribbon lace is still extant, is rare. The fact that it was surrounded by two notebooks, largely containing receipt records, helped to preserve it, as did the specialist care afforded to it from the archives' staff, who initially quarantined it in a freezer to protect it from pests.

Some mystery still surrounds the practice of incorporating shoes into the fabric of a building, which includes placing them under floorboards, in chimneys, fireplaces, walls, ceilings and roofs, and around doors and windows. Whether they served as fertility charms, as perhaps conveyed through the nursery rhyme tale of the 'old woman who lived in a shoe [and] had so many children, she didn't know what to do' is not known. The most accepted theory suggests their use as apotropaic (evil-averting) devices or lucky charms, termed by archaeologists in this context as spiritual middens. Given that shoes – more than any other garment – embody the shape, essence and personality of the wearer, it is thought that they may possess their owner's protective powers; the more well-worn the shoe, the less ambiguous the connection with the original wearer, and the more infused with the owner's good spirit. Alternatively, there are ancient beliefs recounting legends of how witches or devils could be trapped inside shoes, unable to reverse.

DID YOU KNOW?
The Aurora beerhouse, once located at Nos 34-36 Church Street, had the distinction of deploying the town's first automatic flushing toilet. While working efficiently, nevertheless, the Town Council ordered its removal after deeming it wasteful given that its flushing mechanism operated every fifteen minutes, regardless of whether it was used or not.

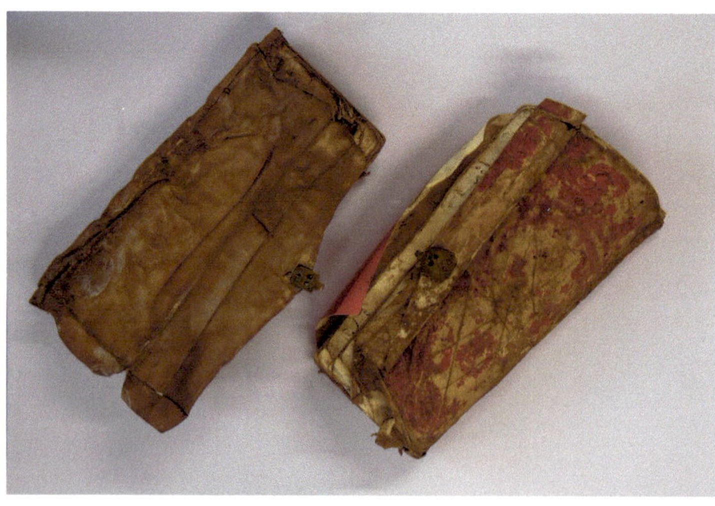

The notebooks, in which the shoe was wrapped.

Whatever the truth, there is irrefutable evidence that many discoveries of shoes remain unreported because of the associated belief that their disturbance may lead to bad luck or that the power of the secret superstition will prove less effective; hence the good fortune that the Tewkesbury example came to light and its importance was recognised. Significantly, the item now features in the nationally important concealed shoe index, maintained by Northampton Museum and Art Gallery, comprising details of around 3,000 shoes.

Enciphered Text

While Tewkesbury has often been associated with Nonconformist groups such as the Religious Society of Friends (Quakers), who faced persecution for their rejection of High Church practices, one religious movement, the Baptists, went to extraordinary lengths to hide their radical beliefs. Originally known as Dissenters, Baptists were viewed with even greater suspicion because of their practice, necessarily carried out in darkness, of immersing adults in water to symbolise the death and resurrection of Christ. In the case of the Tewkesbury Baptists, who met secretly – possibly as early as 1623 – in a fifteenth-century medieval house, converted into a chapel (now restored, with access gained via the John Moore Museum, No. 41 Church Street), it was the 1662 Act of Uniformity, following the restoration of Charles II to the monarchy, that led them to adopt even more covert practices. In April 1663, for example, the group's minute book reveals how the group sought to preserve the anonymity of its members by concealing their names through enciphered text. Nevertheless, this was only required for a short period. From 1689, following the Act of Toleration, the Baptists, like other Nonconformists, were allowed to establish overt places of worship. Consequently, from 1720 the Tewkesbury Baptists began to enhance their chapel building.

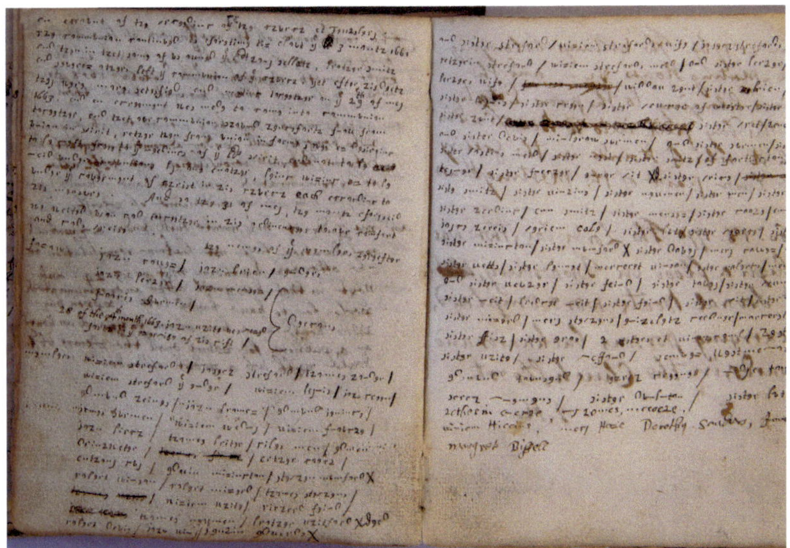

Enciphered text from the Baptist Minute Book 1655 to 1808.

Black Slag Building Blocks

Among the more unusual construction materials, which have occasionally been used in the town, are black slag blocks dating from the eighteenth century. Cast from molten material produced as waste from the copper smelting process, the blocks provided a useful and plentiful source of building material. Originally extracted from Cornish mines, the sulphide ore, then used, generally contained less than 10 per cent of copper, thereby producing much slag for disposal. Although sometimes used in road construction, much of the waste was initially dumped, several Bristol-based smelting works causing navigation problems in the Avon through following this practice. Therefore, its manufacture into building blocks provided a more sustainable long-term solution, its properties making it particularly well suited for use in foundations and as coping stones. The Tewkesbury blocks probably originated in Bristol and may have been used as ballast when ships transported other goods. A survey conducted by the Gloucestershire Society for Industrial Archaeology in 1996–2003 identified examples in the Old Girls' High School wall in Gander Lane and in the quay wall east of the Mill Avon. It is also thought that the quoins used in a house fronting the Avon in St Mary's Road comprise black slag.

Tewkesbury's Antarctic Dog

Raymond Priestley (1886–1974), Tewkesbury's celebrated Antarctic explorer and geologist, returned home on 16 May 1913 after undertaking one of his most perilous expeditions in the southern continent. Among the members of the welcoming party was a Siberian dog called Glennie Nos (derived from his original Russian name Glinie), also known as Long Nose. A few weeks earlier Glennie Nos had taken up residence in Tewkesbury, probably at Stonemason's Yard, Mill Street, where, it is known, he was cared for by Alfred Haines, one of Priestley's relatives, who exercised the dog daily on the Ham.

Glennie Nos was one of thirty-three Siberian sledging dogs recruited by Captain Scott's chief dog-handler, Cecil Meares (1877–1937). After being driven across Siberia to Vladivostok the dogs were carried by steamer to Lyttelton, New Zealand, where they underwent training for the *Terra Nova* expedition (1910–13). Said to be the wisest and quietest dog in the pack Glennie Nos proved himself also to be one of the most capable

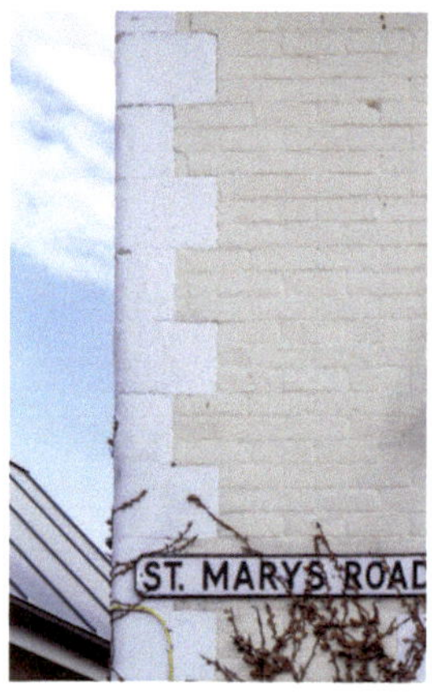

Example of black slag blocks in St Mary's Road.

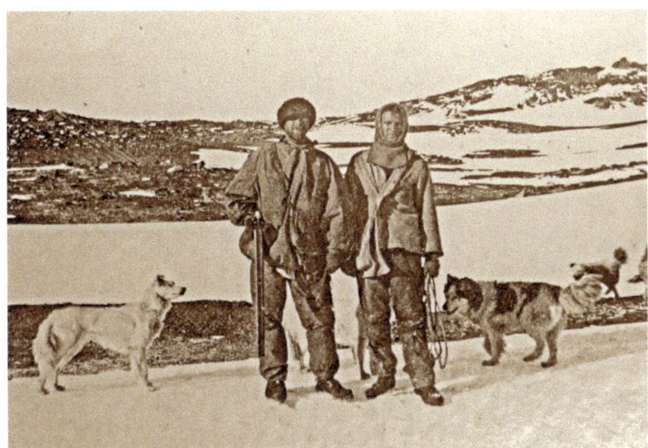

Raymond Priestley (on the left) with dogs in the Antarctic.

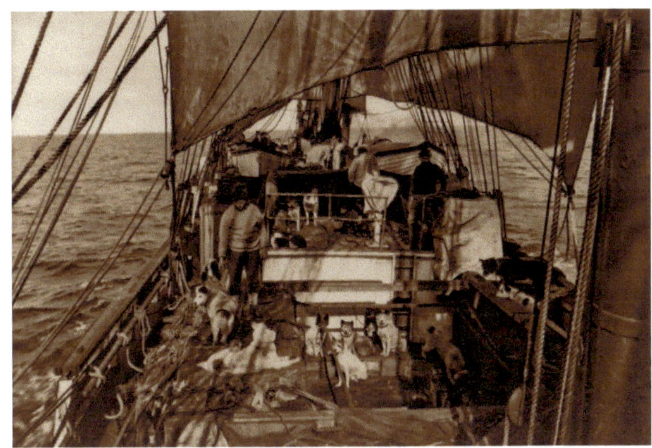

The sled dogs on the deck of the *Terra Nova*, 1910.

and reliable, leading the dogs in Captain Scott's sledge party in October 1911 to the place from where the smaller party then made their final attempt to reach the South Pole. Later, following the tragic death of Captain Scott and his fellow explorers, Glennie Nos led the dogs as part of the search party commanded by the expedition surgeon Edward Atkinson (1881–1929). They discovered the bodies of Scott, Edward Wilson and 'Birdie' Bowers on 12 November 1912.

DID YOU KNOW?
Although Tewkesbury Abbey avoided destruction during the dissolution after the townsfolk petitioned Henry VIII for permission to purchase it, some of its stones have been reused in other buildings in the town. Some examples, including a small part of the Perpendicular cloister, may be seen in the interior walls of Gupshill Manor public house.

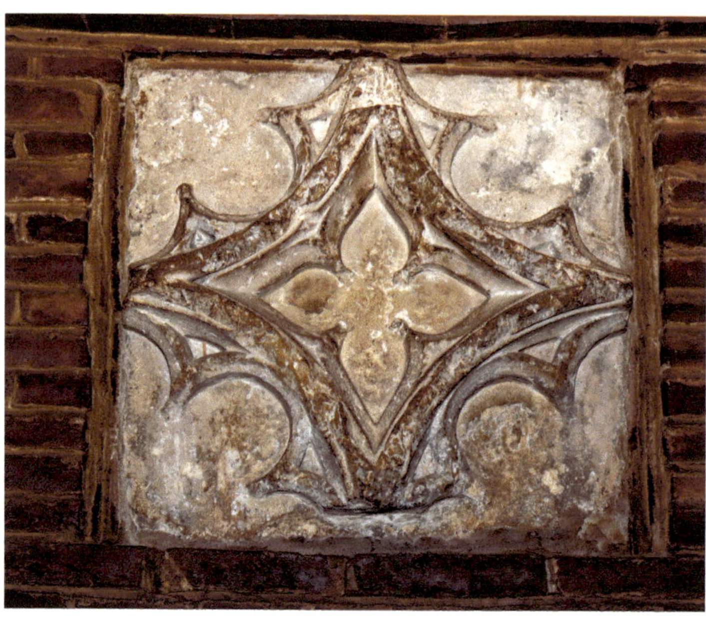

An example of abbey
stonework reset in the
walls of Gupshill Manor.

By then Priestley too had experienced a close encounter with death, having been forced to overwinter in Evans Cove and then traverse 200 miles of sea ice because, earlier, heavy seas had prevented the *Terra Nova* from picking up his team of men. Despite this, Priestley was still able to complete an important ascent and scientific exploration of Mount Erebus, the world's southernmost active volcano. In February 1913 Priestley returned with the *Terra Nova* to Lyttlelton where he was in charge of caring for the surviving dogs. Having chosen to look after Glennie Nos, Priestley put him on the SS *Remeura*, which arrived in London on 17 April, having been a constant companion for Edward Wilson's widow, Oriana, during the long voyage.

Thereafter, Priestley ensured Glennie Nos was well cared for. For a while, Priestley's father looked after him, while he served as headmaster at Tewkesbury Boys' Grammar School. However, following his retirement the dog transferred back into Raymond's personal care who, by now, was receiving signals training at the army centre at Fenny Stanton in Bedfordshire. Consequently, Glennie Nos joined the army, and had the distinction of serving under one Sergeant Butcher. Despite having survived extreme Antarctic conditions and other hardships, including the risk of deadly diseases and the threat of being killed for food, Glennie Nos faced one final challenge, which he passed with flying colours. Following an army decree to destroy dogs of this type, Glennie Nos learned to hide when visiting strangers approached. Such was Priestley's love and respect for this remarkable dog, that when Glennie Nos eventually passed away, he commissioned a pair of gauntlet mittens to be made from Glennie Nos' pelt. Today, one of these remains a treasured possession of the descendants of Alfred Haines, who still reside near Tewkesbury. Tewkesbury Museum in Barton Street maintains a display of Sir Raymond's career, following an exhibition opened by Prince Philip in 2011.

Select Bibliography

Bennett, James (ed.), *The Tewkesbury Yearly Register and Magazine* vol. 1 (1840) and vol. 2 (1850).

Bennett, James, *The History of Tewkesbury* (Tewkesbury: James Bennett, 1830).

Bulletins No. 1 (1992) to No. 31 (2022) [Annual research bulletin published by Tewkesbury Historical Society].

Dixon, John, *Tewkesbury's Two Forgotten Railways!* (Tewkesbury: Tewkesbury Historical Society, 2018).

Eedle, Sam, 'A Tewkesburian at Trafalgar?', Tewkesbury Historical Society *Bulletin* 14 (2005); 'The Continuing Mystery of William Sandilands', *Bulletin* 15 (2006); 'A Tewkesburian at Trafalgar: A Correspondence', *Bulletin* 22 (2013).

Elder, David, *Literary Tewkesbury* (Tewkesbury: Tewkesbury Historical Society, 2016).

Evans, Jill, *Hanged at Gloucester* (Stroud: History Press, 2011).

Hilton, Charles, *A Short History of the Mythe* (Tewkesbury: Charles Hilton, 1985).

Jones, Anthea, *Tewkesbury* (Chichester: Phillimore, 1987).

Linnell, B. R., *Tewkesbury Pubs* (Cheltenham: Theoc Press, 1996, 2nd ed.).

Rogers, John, *A Short History of the Alleys, Courts and Lanes of Tewkesbury* (Tewkesbury: Tewkesbury Museum, 2021, 3rd ed.).

Ross, Kathleen, *The Book of Tewkesbury* (Buckingham: Barracuda Books, 1986).

Tewkesburian [P. Day], *They Used to Live in Tewkesbury* (Stroud: Alan Sutton, 1991).

Willavoys, David, *Tewkesbury Gaol and Its Inhabitants*: *Paper Delivered at Tewkesbury Museum, 22 January 2005* (Tewkesbury: Tewkesbury Museum, 2005)

Woodard database [about 85,000 records available to members and maintained by Tewkesbury Historical Society]

Acknowledgements

I would like to acknowledge the considerable kindness of numerous individuals who have assisted in the production of this book. Particular thanks are due to John Dixon and Jill Waller for reviewing my draft text. They also contributed some of their research, John Dixon providing input on the tanneries and swimming sections, and Jill Waller on the Walton House spa. I am also grateful for other valuable assistance from Anne Careless, Sam Eedle, Steve Goodchild, Margaret Lucas, Joanne Raywood, Sue Webb, and Ray Wilson. Likewise, I am grateful for the support received from the following institutions, including through granting permission to take photographs: Dean Close School Archives, Gloucestershire Archives, Gloucestershire Library Services and Gloucestershire Police Archives. I would also like to thank the following who kindly supplied the following images: Ghent University Library for p. 9 (*Histoire de la rentrée victorieuse du roi Edouard IV en son royaume d'Angleterre, 1471*) [BHSL.HS.0236]; Tewkesbury Historical Society for Charles Alban Buckler image of Abbey p. 8; Shakespeare Folger Library for p. 46 and p. 77; Wellcome Collection for p. 13, p. 18, p. 28, p. 32, p. 40, p. 48, p. 50, p. 53 and p. 78; Mary J Lillistone for p. 88 (middle and bottom); John Dixon and Roger Carver for p. 61; John Dixon and Rosemary Wherrett for p. 64 (top); John Dixon for p. 73 (bottom); David Postle and the Kidderminster Railway Museum for p. 62; Gloucestershire Police Archives for p. 38 (bottom) and p. 41; Gloucestershire Archives for p. 24, p. 37, p. 38 (top), p. 86 (top), p. 89, p. 90 and p. 91; Cheltenham College Archives for p. 67;and the Library of Congress for p. 29, p. 84 and p. 93 (bottom). I am also grateful to Graham Downie, chair of the John Moore Society, for permission to reproduce the extract from *Tewkesbury: My Favourite Town*. While every effort has been made to contact all copyright owners, if any have been overlooked I apologise and will seek to rectify matters. Finally, my heartfelt thanks to my family, Meg, Rachel and Catrin, for their patience, understanding and support.